"Representative government is the subject of this little book by the Virginia gentleman who was the fifth President of the United States. A State's sovereign and a State's government must not be identical, if order and freedom and justice are to prevail: that is the lesson which James Monroe teaches through first a general analysis and then a comparison of the American republic with the Athenian, Spartan, and Carthaginian republics....

"Monroe feared that at some future time the Federal government might assert itself the sovereign as well—or some branch of the Federal government, or corps within it. Since his time, the division of sovereign powers between Federal and State governments virtually has ceased to exist: the Congress now legislates as if there never had been a doctrine of reserved powers under the Constitution. Yet sovereignty and government are not totally entwined, two centuries after the framing of the Constitution of the United States; and a good many Americans still understand the dangers of plebiscitary democracy....

"James Monroe endeavors to dissuade the sovereign people from creating what Tocqueville would call 'democratic despotism'...; and he cautions ambitious public men not to fancy themselves

(continued on back flap)

THE PEOPLE

THE SOVEREIGNS

FROM THE PORTRAIT BY REMBRANDT PEALE

James Monroe

This portrait of President James Monroe
was painted from life in 1824.
One of only three three-quarter length portraits
painted by Peale (1778-1860), it is
widely judged to be Monroe's
finest portrait and is considered
to be one of the great portraits of the era.

THE PEOPLE

THE SOVEREIGNS

BEING

A COMPARISON OF THE GOVERNMENT OF THE
UNITED STATES WITH THOSE OF THE REPUBLICS
WHICH HAVE EXISTED BEFORE, WITH
THE CAUSES OF THEIR DECADENCE AND FALL

BY JAMES MONROE
Ex-President of the United States

AND

DEDICATED BY THE AUTHOR TO HIS COUNTRYMEN

EDITED BY
SAMUEL L. GOUVERNEUR
HIS GRANDSON AND ADMINISTRATOR

WITH AN INTRODUCTION BY
RUSSELL KIRK

JAMES RIVER PRESS
CUMBERLAND, VIRGINIA 23040
1987

Published by James River Press
Cumberland, Virginia 23040
(804) 492-4949

Originally published: Philadelphia: J.B. Lippincott & Co., 1867.

Library of Congress Cataloging-in-Publication Data

Monroe, James, 1758-1831.
  The people, the sovereigns.
  Includes index.
  1. State, The.   2. United States—Politics and government.
3. Athens (Greece)— Politics and government.   4. Sparta (Ancient
city) Region—Politics and government.   5. Carthage (Ancient city)—
Politics and government.
I. Kirk, Russell.   II. Title.

JC212.M75   1987   320.1   87-3854

ISBN 0-940973-02-2

The paper in this book is acid-free and meets the guidelines for permanence and durability
of the Committee on Production Guidelines for Book Longevity of the Council on Library
Resources.

CONTENTS

CHAPTER I

CHAPTER II

ACKNOWLEDGEMENTS

Many people have helped make the republication of this book possible. Foremost among them is Dr. James McClellan, President of the Center for Judicial Studies, Cumberland, Virginia, and Washington, D.C., under whose guidance the project was conceived and completed. The book is published jointly by the Center and the James Monroe Memorial Foundation. I want also to thank David A. Bovenizer, Associate Editor of the Ethics and Public Policy Center, Washington, D.C., and assistant editor of *Benchmark* for assisting with preparation of the manuscript. Both of these scholars are trustees of the James Monroe Memorial Foundation.

I am especially grateful as well to all of the other Foundation members for their support of this project—Morton Blackwell, Capt. James H. Campbell, Elizabeth Campbell, Clement Conger, Charles Dickens, Col. Samuel T. Dickens, Capt. Miles P. DuVal, Jr., Christopher Honenberger, Pauline Johnson, Dr. James P. Lucier, Mary Grace Lucier, Molly Synon McClellan, Francis Dana Payne, Mrs. James W. Rawles, Roslyn T. Reed, G. William Thomas, and the late Andrew W. Duncan.

Thanks are also due to trustees of the Center for Judicial Studies, who include my colleagues Ralph Husted, Thomas Pauken, Alfred S. Regnery, Clyde Sluhan, and W.D. Stedman.

The Hon. Helen Marie Taylor
U.S. Representative to the United Nations, 1986–87

President, James Monroe Memorial Foundation
Chairman of the Board, Center for Judicial Studies

INTRODUCTION

by Russell Kirk

REPRESENTATIVE government is the subject of this little book by the Virginia gentleman who was the fifth President of the United States. A State's sovereign and a State's government must not be identical, if order and freedom and justice are to prevail: that is the lesson which James Monroe teaches through first a general analysis and then a comparison of the American republic with the Athenian, Spartan, and Carthaginian republics.

Monroe was near his end when, between 1825 and 1831, he wrote this earnest study, which he never completed; he had intended, should he live long enough, to include examinations of the Roman Republic and the British Constitution. (That last comparison would have been especially interesting, no doubt.) It was not until 1867 that *The People the Sovereigns* was published, and few scholars in American politics or history then or since have commented upon this treatise.

"The name of James Monroe has yet to receive the exalted appreciation which it deserves, and which posterity surely will award." So Hugh Blair Grigsby said in 1854, in his discourse *The Virginia Convention of 1829–30*. Thirteen decades later, Monroe remains somewhat neglected, perhaps because his presidential years were the Era of Good Feeling, with little heated partisanship to enliven political history. Yet he was a public man of much successful experience, thoughtful and popular, and as President "the first incumbent of the chair since Washington filled it, who had seen the flash of a hostile gun, and had drawn his sword in defense of his country." His final public service was to preside over Virginia's Constitutional Convention in 1829, with Madison, Marshall, and John Randolph among the delegates; but his health was too feeble for him to complete his task; he withdrew from the Convention and died at New York on July 4, 1831. The Monroe Doctrine is his memorial.

Written in praise of the American democratic republic, *The People the Sovereigns* took form in old Monroe's mind only a few years before Tocqueville so brilliantly analyzed American institutions; because we now think of the American Republic in Tocqueville's phrases and see democracy through his eyes, we may find Monroe's concepts and style somewhat archaic, almost as if they belonged to the era of George III and Louis XV. His historical method, drawing from Aristotle and Polybius and Plutarch, is very like that of John Adams' *Defence of the Constitutions of Government of the United States of America*, which had been written on the eve of the Constitutional Convention of 1787. Monroe's was the last voice of the Revolutionary generation.

This notwithstanding, *The People the Sovereigns* remains worth reading, and not only because it is that rare thing—a philosophical discourse from the pen of a President of the United States. For it is an essay in intelligent praise of the American Constitution, as seen four decades after the Convention at Philadelphia. Monroe in effect warns Americans against excessive concentration of power in the government, and against the fancy that an abstract Popular Will may direct the courses of great states. Confusion about the relationships between sovereignty and government worked the ruin of Athens, Sparta, and Carthage, he argues; and he implies that the Constitution of the United States must be cherished as the best instrument ever devised for reconciling popular sovereignty with energetic government for the common good.

Monroe's terms *sovereignty* and *people* require some explanation. John Austin's dull but influential book *The Providence of Jurisprudence Determined*, on which has hinged for the past century and a quarter most discussion of the concept of sovereignty, would be published merely a year after Monroe's death—although nobody paid attention to Austin's treatise until the 1860s. Nor was Monroe influenced by Jeremy Bentham's *Fragment on Government* (1776), which for the most part is an assault on earlier concepts of sovereignty. Unaffected by the arguments of the Benthamites and the Analytical Jurists, James Madison understood *sovereignty* much as Sir William Blackstone had expounded it. With Blackstone, Monroe regards sovereignty as a political and ethical matter, rather than a legal problem.

More specifically, we can apprehend Monroe on sovereignty by turning to James Otis' pamphlet *The Rights of the British Colonies Asserted and Proved*—published at Boston in 1764, when James Monroe was six years old. This passage from Otis eloquently expresses the Patriot's grasp of the idea of sovereignty, which Monroe would reaffirm as a theory more than sixty years later:

"An original, supreme, absolute, and uncontrollable earthly power must exist in and preside over every society, from whose final decisions there can be no appeal but directly to Heaven. It is, therefore, originally and ultimately in the people; . . . and [they] never did in fact freely, nor can they rightfully, make an absolute unlimited renunciation of this divine right. It is ever in the nature of the thing given in trust, and on a condition the performance of which no mortal can dispense with, namely, that the person or persons on whom the sovereignty is conferred by the people, shall incessantly consult their good.''

Monroe, differing in some degree from Otis, would reason that *power*, rather than *sovereignty*, was conferred upon governors by the sovereign people. But otherwise Monroe holds that concept of sovereignty to which Patriot spokesmen appealed from 1764 to 1775. Its source may be found in Sir Matthew Hale and Sir Edward Coke; even in Richard Hooker; in the English medieval principal that ''the king is under the law.'' Monroe's doctrine of sovereignty was rooted in English historical experience, rather than in juridical abstractions.

Against this theory of popular sovereignty was set the despotic, or mechanical, concept of sovereignty, first clearly declared by Jean Bodin, in 1576—representing the prince as the possessor of total sovereignty. When Monroe was eight years old, Louis XV thrust that definition upon the Parlement of Paris:

''Sovereignty lies in me alone. The legislative power is mine unconditionally and indivisibly. The public order emanates from me, and I am its supreme guardian. My people is one with me.''

This later concept of sovereignty has prevailed in most of the world, since 1918: not the sovereignty of the house of Bourbon, of course, but the glowering absolutism of the totalist states, admitting no appeal against the authority of the fanatic political regime, in which sovereign and government are indistinguishable. The old Prince—curbed in exercising sovereignty by the influence of religion and custom—has been supplanted by the new Party, for whom ideology justifies every atrocity. Monroe was not mistaken in predicting that despotism would rise again in many lands should sovereignty and government be confounded.

As for ''the People,'' Monroe is imprecise in definition. When minister to revolutionary France, Monroe had addressed the National Convention, and there had been fraternally embraced; but he was no leveller. He had told Virginia's House of Delegates in 1809, and Virginia's Constitutional Convention in 1829, of his witnessing in Paris ''the murder of a member in the midst of the French National Convention by a mob which marched among the members with the severed head of their victim stuck upon a pole'' (Grigsby's words); his notion of ''the People'' did not at all resemble Sansculotte. No, when Monroe writes ''the People'' he means what was meant in 1787 and 1788, when the authors of *The Federalist* and the more eminent framers of the Constitution had occasion to refer to the people as "the only legitimate fountain of power." As R. M. MacIver wrote half a century ago, at the Constitutional Convention, "the people are not to be construed as Rousseau's 'people,' the totality of component human beings expressing their sovereign will. There was besides the nice question whether the slaves should be counted as persons . . . . The whole body of citizens must be the final arbiter of government, but under such conditions as to check what Alexander Hamilton called 'the imprudence of democracy.'"

By 1829, Monroe was not so contemptuous of democracy as Hamilton had been at the Convention in 1787; but he had his misgivings about democratic impulse at the Virginia Convention over which he presided. Monroe's "People," embodied, would have been an orderly assembly of substantial Virginian farmers, the constituency of the Virginia dynasty of Presidents. Burke had written in 1790 that the true English people consisted of some four hundred thousand men, qualified in one way or another to form sensible opinions and take some part in public affairs. For Monroe, as for Burke, the Mob was not the People.

James Monroe knew that it is altogether possible for the majority in a nation to become a great beast—supposing that the people should endeavor to make themselves the government, despite their being the sovereigns. "While it is known that the government of an individual, in which the people have no participation, is despotic," Monroe writes, "it might be inferred that that which passed to the opposite extreme, in which the whole power was vested in, and exercised by, the people collectively, was the most free and the best that human wisdom could devise. If men were angels, that result would follow, but in that case, there would be no necessity for any government. It is the knowledge that all men have weaknesses, and that many have vices, that makes government necessary; and in adopting one, it is the interest of all that it should be formed in such a manner as to protect the rights and promote the happiness of the whole community. The great object is to promote the celestial cause of liberty and humanity; and the perfection of government must consist in its being formed in such a manner as to accomplish this object, by depriving the vicious of the power to do harm, and enlisting not the virtuous only, but all who are not abandoned and outlawed, in support of the government thus instituted."

A despotism or an aristocracy, exercising sovereignty and at the same time directing the government, will fall into injustice and resist public liberty; but a democracy may be no better, unless it separates sovereignty from government. How may this be accomplished?

Why, by arranging that the sovereign people delegate certain powers to their agents, for the common good: that is, the government must not be sovereign, but merely representative of the people, who do not surrender their sovereignty to executive, legislative, or judicial branches of the government. Attempts by the people to govern directly failed miserably in ancient times, and must fail always: those sovereigns, the people, cannot act wisely, as a mass, upon prudential concerns—whatever demagogues may tell them. Let sovereignty and government exist in symbiosis, well distinguished one from the other; union of the two brings popular servitude. His models for the commonwealth are the constitutions of the United States and of the several States. The functions of sovereignty are divided between the Federal structure and the several States; so Monroe would have the Union remain. In revolutionary France, "the government was in effect united with the sovereignty in the people, and all power, legislative, executive, and judicial, concentrated in them." That terrible error had not taken hold in the United States.

Monroe commends bicameral legislatures, the stern restraining power of impeachment, an independent judiciary, and especially the doctrine and practice of the separation of powers—all features of American constitutions. These are successful devices for separating sovereignty and government. It would have been interesting to read him on British constitutional developments during his own time: for cabinet government through responsible party, as contrasted with the separation of powers among executive, legislative, and judicial branches, was then taking form in Britain. But his reflections on that subject, together with his analysis of the Roman constitution, never were set down on paper.

In portions of this treatise, Monroe displays noticeable independence and originality—particularly in his seven-page criticism of John Locke. It has been a curiously shallow assumption of many American historians, for a long while, that Locke's thought dominated the men of 1776 and the men of 1787. Actually, Blackstone, Hume, and Burke were stronger influences upon leading Americans of that age than was Locke; and the Constitution was founded not upon philosophers' theories, but upon colonial and British experience of political order. Although Monroe approves with some reservations Locke's championing of "the rights of the people," he dissents from Locke's allowing the executive to fix the number of representatives; he argues that Locke "says nothing in favor of the independence of the judiciary," and allows judges no power to rule upon constitutionality. Little can be found in Locke except for Locke's general commendation of liberty, Monroe remarks, that is applicable to the United

States. Locke's *Second Treatise of Civil Government*, Monroe concludes, was well enough for its time; but "He does not look at the dangers to which our system is exposed, nor suggest the means of averting them."

Monroe feared that at some future time the Federal government might assert itself the sovereign as well—or some branch of the Federal government, or corps within it. Since his time, the division of sovereign powers between Federal and State governments virtually has ceased to exist: the Congress now legislates as if there never had been a doctrine of reserved powers under the Constitution. Yet sovereignty and government are not totally entwined, two centuries after the framing of the Constitution of the United States; and a good many Americans still understand the dangers of plebiscitary democracy.

In one respect, Monroe failed to discern the future of the balancing of powers within the Federal government. "For the judiciary to make encroachments on either of the branches seems to be impossible," he writes, "the nature of its powers and duties being so different and obvious." It would go otherwise in the latter half of the twentieth century, when the reproach of "judicial usurpation" would be flung at the Supreme Court again and again, with reason. Monroe, unlike Jefferson, foresaw no such conflict; of the power of the Supreme Court to find acts of the Congress or of the executive branch unconstitutional, he wrote complacently, "The exercise of the proposed power by the judiciary, could never involve the question of conflicting rights between it and the legislature, in the character of encroachment on those of the latter. In exercising that power, the judiciary could be viewed only as a tribunal of the people, invested with it, to prevent encroachments, tending to subvert the Constitution, and with it, their rights and liberties." Monroe labored under various apprehensions as to the future, but never could he have fancied that one day the Supreme Court might forbid prayer in public schools, or declare the inalienable right of women to destroy their progeny in the womb.

Behind the doctrine of popular sovereignty there lurks sometimes the intolerant heresy of *vox populi vox dei*; and as an antidote to extravagant populism, it is well to read Sir Osbert Sitwell's long poem *Demos the Emperor*. In this small book, James Monroe endeavors to dissuade the sovereign people from creating what Tocqueville would call "democratic despotism" (a concept one finds, in nearly that phrase, in Monroe's pages); and he cautions ambitious public men not to fancy themselves sovereign. As the American Republic enters its third century, such injunctions ought not to be ignored.

PREFACE

THE following work was written by Mr. Monroe between the years 1825, when he retired from the Presidency, and 1831, that of his death. In a letter, now before me, dated April 8, 1830, to an old friend, he says: "I have composed in part another work[1]—a comparison between our government and that of the Ancient Republics. Of this, I have already extended it to a view of Lacedemon, of Greece, and of Carthage, to which I have drawn an Introductory view of Government and Society, as the basis of the work. This I could also finish in about the same time by devoting myself to it." The work, as it came into my hands, was in its rough and incomplete state; I have reflected upon it for years, and after considerable time and labor have joined its several parts together, until it comprises the whole as it now stands. Not one word has been added to the original text, neither has one been erased from the manuscript copy.

These few words are deemed necessary by way of explanation, in order that any apparent omissions,[2] defects or errors, might be pardoned by those to whom the work is dedicated, as the Author had no opportunity to revise and correct, and the Editor has not presumed to exercise any critical interpolation of its contents. Before publication, the work was submitted to some of the most distinguished literary gentlemen of the country, including the Hon. George Bancroft, the American Historian, and Mr. Samuel Tyler, known in the United States and Europe from his Philosophical Writings; and the Editor has been encouraged by them to give it to the world, incomplete as it is. The style and language of the work are plain, in character with the man who wrote it, and of his countrymen, to whom it is addressed. The People, whom he considers the originators and supporters of all Governments, and the Sovereigns in the exercise of the Powers of Government—(this being the true exposition of the Monroe Doctrine)—

---

[1] The other manuscript papers of Mr. Monroe were purchased in 1849, by the Congress of the United States, and are now among the Archives of the Department of State, Washington City.

[2] The author intended, judging from notes found with the papers, to have also instituted a comparison with the Roman Republic and the Government of Great Britain, but owing to advanced age and declining health, failed to do so.

will, I trust, as a voice of warning from the past, comprehend its precepts. That its teachings may be salutary, and that they may profit by the lessons the treatise inculcates, is the sincere wish and hope of

SAMUEL L. GOUVERNEUR
1867

BIOGRAPHICAL SKETCH OF
THE AUTHOR

JAMES, the son of Spence Monroe, was born on the banks of the Potomac River, in the County of Westmoreland, Virginia. He was descended from Hector Monroe, an officer of the army of Charles the First, who emigrated with other cavaliers to Virginia, after the battle of Marston Moor in 1644, and at the time of his birth his father resided on the original grant to his ancestor. His education was commenced at a classical school in the county, superintended by the Rev. Mr. Campbell. At the age of sixteen, he was entered at William and Mary's College.[3]" The opportunities it afforded for liberal instruction were great; here he pursued his studies until 1776, when the college was partially closed by the preparation for the Revolutionary War. The same feeling which animated the Fathers of American Liberty, gradually diffused among those who were to constitute the next generation, had penetrated the halls of learning, and was rapidly converting the sons of science into the youthful and enthusiastic champions of their country's rights and honors. Partaking in a high degree of the spirit which pervaded the Colony of Virginia, James Monroe and John Francis Mercer, early and steadfast friends through life, both at the age of eighteen years, with others of high claims to merit, abandoned their literary pursuits, and devoted themselves entirely to the military service of their country, entering as Cadets in the 3d Virginia Regiment. It was raised and then commanded by Col. Hugh Mercer of that state, soon after appointed a Brigadier-General. He was soon after appointed a Lieutenant and ordered to the army under George Washington. The same year he led his company in the battle of Harlem Heights and White Plains, and was with the army in their retreat through the Jerseys. At the battle of Trenton, perceiving that the enemy were placing in position a battery to rake the American line, he gallantly advanced at the head of a small detachment, charged the battery, drove the artillerymen from their guns, and took possession of them.

In this engagement he received a ball in the shoulder, which he carried to his grave, and having attracted the attention of his superior officers by

---

[3]Memoir of James Monroe, in Department of State, Washington.

his quickness of perception, and gallantry on the occasion, was immediately promoted to a Captaincy. While scarcely recovered and suffering from his wound, he was offered and accepted the appointment of Aide-de-Camp on the Staff of Lord Stirling with the rank of Major, and served in that capacity during the campaigns of 1777 and 1778, distinguishing himself for zeal and gallantry at the battles of Brandywine and Germantown, and was by the side of Lafayette when the latter was wounded at Monmouth.

By the acceptance of the position of Aide-de-Camp to Lord Stirling, he lost his rank in the regular line of the Army; and General Washington, who at that early period entertained a high opinion of his abilities, recommended him to the Legislature of Virginia for a command in one of the new regiments to be raised in that state. The appointment of Lieutenant-Colonel was accordingly conferred upon him. He immediately commenced action, looking to the organization and recruiting of the regiment to the command of which he was assigned. But finding after a time, from the exhausted condition of the state, all his efforts at success fruitless, he retired as supernumerary officer.

Returning to Richmond, Virginia, he commenced the study of the law under Mr. Jefferson, then Governor of Virginia, devoting himself more especially to the study of topographical law. At this period he corresponded with some of the most distinguished men in the Colonies; and among others, General Charles Lee, who resided in Berkeley County, living in retirement almost isolated from the world. In a letter to this erratic but distinguished general, he complains of the lack of books to pursue his studies. To this, General Lee replies in a characteristic letter, dated June 25, 1780, urging him to cultivate the talents with which nature had gifted him, and stating his views in relation to the aspects of affairs generally "on the Continent."

GENERAL CHARLES LEE TO JAMES MONROE.

BERKELEY COUNTY, *June ye 25th,* 1780.
MY DEAR MONROE:—

I received two days ago your letter dated from Richmond upbraiding me for not writing. I do assure you that I have written twice immediately addressed to you, and a third time addressed to you conjointly with Mercer; but, whether you have received them I cannot say, as amongst the many admirable qualities pervading the inhabitants of this Continent, the noble ambition of opening every letter, in order to obtain knowledge, is one of the most predominant; it is not always that I am master of pen, ink and paper, and seldom that I have an opportunity of assuring you how much and sincerely I am yours, or you may depend on it that you should receive these assurances very frequently, as without compliment there are few young men for whom I have a higher esteem and affection. I am extremely concerned that Fortune has been so unkind as not to admit of your cultivating the talents which nature has bestowed on you to greater advantage than your present situation seems to promise, for in my opinion (but perhaps I am a prejudiced man) the study of topographical law (unless daily corrected by other more liberal studies) is a most horrid narrower of the mind; and you, as you justly complain, have not the proper books for this necessary correction. If I remain on the Continent, nothing will give me greater pleasure, or more flatter my ambition than to communicate my ideas and assist you with all the means in my power in your pursuit of private letters, and if any circumstances arise to make me alter my present plan, I hope it may be so contrived that we may be much together. Your present assembly I have many reasons to believe is composed of most wretched materials; but wretched as it is, I have as many reasons to believe, that it is one of the least abominable on the Continent; in fact the power in every state is fallen into the very worst hands. We have now neither Monarchy, Aristocracy, nor Democracy; if it is anything, it is rather Mac-oc-racy, by which I mean that a banditti of low Scotch Irish who are either themselves imported servants, or the immediate descendants of imported servants are the lords paramount, and in such wild beastly hands as these *respublica diutius stare non potest,* God knows what is to become of us; I possibly see with a jaundiced eye, but I am myself fully persuaded that after some months, or at farthest a couple of years' anarchy and confusion, an absolute tyranny will be the conclusion of the piece; but whether the tyrant will be foreign or domestick is out of the reach of my foresight. What do you think of the policy or virtue of Congress, in inviting, or if not invited, in admitting a large body of French troops into our bosom? How are we to get rid of 'em? Is there an instance in the history of a strong nation sending an army for the protection of an impotent one, when the protectors have not ultimately stripped or attempted to strip the protected of their liberties?

You have, I am sure, read the history of Britain, and must be acquainted with the conduct of our Saxon ancestors. You have likewise probably read the history of Charles the Fifth and Philip the Second, and of course must know that armies of Germans, Italians, and Spaniards, introduced under the pretext of protecting the low countries against the French, were employed to enslave these very low countries, and that afterwards, *vice versa*, the French call'd in to protect 'em from the tyranny of the Spaniards and Italians, attempted to accomplish the very same purposes they were called in to defeat—in short the measure is so very big with mischief, so repugnant to the first axioms of policy, that I cannot persuade myself but that those who have acquiesced must have been bribed out of the little sense they set out with; but I am warmed by the subject into a tedious political essay; it has been revealed to Mrs. Gates in a dream that South Carolina is not of the least importance, which revelation she has communicated to the general to his unspeakable comfort; the general has communicated it to a McAllaster and the other commissioners, who have comforted the whole country with the glad tidings, and it is resolved by a committee of Whigs, that whoever insinuates that South Carolina and the army taking it are of the least consequence, is *ipso facto* a damn'd Tory—upon my word I pity Gates, he is an honest man, and has many good qualities, and that demoness, his wife, occasions him to make a very ridiculous figure. Adieu. God bless you.

C. Lee.

P.S. I suppose an army of Russians will likewise be introduced as well as an army of French, and then the Continent will be a blessed theatre of war and desolation; one side or other must be victorious, or it must be a drawn battle; if the former happens, the victor will dictate what measures he pleases, and if the latter happens, a treaty of partition will take place— upon the whole it is a damnable measure.

The enemy, however, soon after appearing in this state, he exerted himself in the organization of the militia of the lower counties; but upon their retiring soon after, by direction of Governor Jefferson he proceeded as military commissioner to the army in the South. Cornwallis having surrendered at Yorktown, he returned to Richmond. In 1782 he was elected to the Assembly, and although but in the twenty-third year of his age, elected a member of the executive council. In 1783 he was elected to Congress for the term of three years, where in 1785, he offered a resolution that Congress be authorized to regulate trade between the states. This resolution was referred to a committee of which he was chairman, and reported upon favorably; and led, it is said, to the Convention at Annapolis, and the adoption of the Federal Constitution. He was appointed member of the commission to settle the controversy in relation to the boundary between Massachusetts and New York. He strongly opposed the demand of Spain for a relinquishment of the right to navigate the Mississippi River. Having served out his term in Congress, and being ineligible for the next three years, he returned to Virginia with his wife, Miss Kortright of New York, whom he had married the previous year, and established himself in the practice of the law at Fredericksburg. In 1787 he was again elected to the General Assembly of Virginia, and in 1788 was chosen a delegate to the Virginia Convention, to decide upon the adoption of the Federal Constitution. In 1790 he became a member of the United States Senate. In 1794 he was appointed Minister to France, and was recalled in 1796. In 1799 he was elected Governor of Virginia. In 1803 he was appointed Envoy Extraordinary to negotiate, in conjunction with the Minister Resident, Mr. Livingston, for the purchase of Louisiana. The result exceeded his most sanguine expectations. Within a fortnight after his arrival in Paris, for the sum of fifteen millions of dollars, the entire "Territory of Orleans, District of Louisiana," comprising a larger extent of country than the then whole United States, was added to the territory of the Union. In 1803 he was appointed Minister Plenipotentiary to England. When in the midst of the negotiations pending for the protection of neutral rights, and against the impressment of seamen, he was directed to proceed to Madrid, as Minister Extraordinary and Plenipotentiary to adjust the boundaries of the purchase of Louisiana. In 1806 he was recalled to England, to act with Mr. Pinkney in the negotiation for the protection of neutral rights. In 1810 he was again elected to the General Assembly of Virginia, and in 1811 again chosen governor of the state. In the same year he was appointed by President Madison Secretary of State; and on the resignation of the War Department by General Armstrong, after the capture of Washington, at the earnest solicitation of Mr. Madison, he also took charge of the administration of that department, performing the duties of both of these laborious and important branches of the government. While in the performance of these double functions, he refused to accept the higher salary of Secretary of State, receiving only that of Secretary of War, and the difference between the two rates of pay, over $2,000, remained on the books of the Treasury Department to his credit, until the year 1849, when it was claimed and paid to his executor. Retiring from the Department of War, on the conclusion of peace, he continued to serve as Secretary of State until the end of Mr. Madison's administration in 1817. In that year he succeeded to the Presidency with Daniel D. Tompkins for Vice-President. Among the important public events which marked his first term as President, were the admission of the states of Illinois, Mississippi, and Maine. In 1818 a Convention was concluded between Great Britain and the United States, in relation to the Newfoundland fisheries and other objects. In 1819 Spain ceded to the United States the Floridas. In 1820 he and Mr. Tompkins were again nominated and elected; the former by a vote of 231 out of 232, there being but one vote against him in the Electoral College; the latter by a vote of 218. In 1820 Missouri was admitted into the Union. In 1822 the independence of Mexico and the South American Provinces was recognized. On the 2d of December, 1823, he sent to Congress a Message on the policy of neither entangling ourselves in the broils of Europe, nor suffering the powers of the Old World to interfere with the New, known as the Monroe Doctrine. He declared that any attempt on the part of the European Powers "to extend their system to any portion of this hemisphere" would be regarded by the United States "as dangerous to our peace and safety." In 1824 General Lafayette visited the United States, and for a time was the guest of Mr. Monroe, at his residence, Oak Hill, Loudon County, Virginia. He was subsequently chosen a Justice of the Peace; was elected one of the Board of Visitors of the University of Virginia, and in 1829 became a member of the Virginia Convention, to revise the Constitution of that state, and was chosen to preside over their deliberations. In 1831, whilst on a visit to his younger daughter in the City of New York, he was taken ill and died, like his predecessors, Adams and Jefferson, on the 4th of July, the anniversary of the Declaration of Independence of the country to whose service he had devoted the chief portion of his life, at the age of seventy-four years. On the 2d of July, 1858, his remains, escorted by a grand military and civil procession, were removed from the vault where they had lain for twenty-seven years, to the steamer Jamestown, on which they were conveyed to Richmond, arriving on the 5th of July, and were escorted by the military and civil authorities to Hollywood Cemetery, where they were finally interred, in the one hundredth year from the date of his birth. His epitaph is unwritten, his eulogy in the words of John Quincy Adams:—

"Mr. Monroe strengthened his country for defense by a system of combined fortifications, military and naval, sustaining her rights, her dignity, and honor abroad, soothing her dissensions, and conciliating her acerbities at home; controlling by a firm though peaceful policy the hostile spirit of European alliance against republican South America; extorting by the mild compulsion of reason, the shores of the Pacific from the stipulated acknowledgment of Spain; and leading back the Imperial Autocrat of the North to his lawful boundaries, from his hastily asserted dominion over the Southern Ocean. Thus strengthening and consolidating the federative edifice of his country's union, till he was entitled to say, like Augustus Caesar, of his imperial city, that he had found her built of brick, and left her constructed of marble.''

CHAPTER I

A COMPARATIVE ELEMENTARY VIEW OF
GOVERNMENT AND OF SOCIETY

HAVING served my country, from very early life, in its most important trusts, abroad and at home, my mind has been turned in the discharge of my public duties to the principles of the system itself, in the success of which I have taken, and always shall take, a deep interest. I have witnessed our difficulties, and have seen with delight the virtue and talent by which they were surmounted. In looking to our future progress, some important questions occur to which great attention is due. Are we not still menaced with dangers? Of what nature are they and to what cause or causes imputable? To these objects my mind has also been drawn with great interest; and having now leisure, it is my intention to express my sentiments freely on them, in the hope that I may thereby render some service, and under the conviction that in those instances in which I may err I shall do no harm.

It has been often affirmed that our Revolution forms the most important epoch in the history of mankind, and in this sentiment I fully concur. But whence does it derive its importance? The sentiment is founded in a belief that it has introduced a system of new governments better calculated to secure to the people the blessings of liberty, and under circumstances more favorable to success, than any which the world ever knew before. If such be the fact, the truth of the affirmation must be conceded, for surely no event can be so important, as the establishment of a new system of government, which by its intrinsic merit, and the force of example, promises to promote so essentially the happiness of mankind.

Other republics have failed. Their career, though brilliant, was marked by contentions which frequently convulsed and finally overthrew them. To what causes were those contentions imputable? Was it that the governments respectively were so defective that their failure was inevitable? Or were the societies, of which those republics were composed, incapable of such governments? To one or other of those causes, or to a combination of them, their fate must have been imputable. Do like causes exist here?

1

If they do, it follows that we are exposed in a certain degree at least to a like fate. These are fair objects of inquiry, and I propose to inquire into them.

To present in a clear and distinct light the difference between the governments and people of the United States, and those of other countries, ancient and modern, and to show that certain causes which produced disastrous effects in them do not exist in most instances, and are inapplicable in all, to ours, is an inquiry of great extent, if pursued in all its parts. It involves all the great principles of free government, with a comparative view of their respective merits, and likewise of the society, regarding the state in which it may be, over which such government is established. The subject, nevertheless, admits of great condensation, without impairing its necessary illustration. The questions to be solved are, have we so far avoided the errors and corrected the defects of other free governments, as to have attained a degree of perfection which was unknown to them? Are our societies in a state better adapted to the support of such governments, than those of any other people ever were, over whom such governments were established? If we have been thus blessed, it must follow that the example of other republics cannot touch ours, and that we have just cause to calculate on a destiny altogether different from that which befell other people, even those who were most free. We shall have gained an eminence, which no other nation ever reached, and from which, if we fall, the fault will be in ourselves, and we shall thereby give the most discouraging example to mankind that the world ever witnessed.

To do justice to the subject, we must not only go to first principles, but trace all the causes which bear on them to their source. If a people be free and their government be defective, why do they not amend it? As the injury arising from the defects of the government must be felt in its operation, and the defects be in consequence, apparent, it is strange having the power exclusively in their hands, if they do not amend them. And if the people participate only in the government, by the occupation of any strong and independent ground in the system, it cannot but excite surprise, having numbers and force on their side, if they should be driven from it; if instead of improving their position, they should lose it altogether. However defective, therefore, the government of the ancient republics may have been, it is obvious that their overthrow could not have been imputable to those defects only; that it may be traced in part at least, to a higher source, to the people themselves. No people blessed with liberty could be deprived of it, if they were not made dupes and the instruments of their own destruction. If they possessed the necessary intelligence and virtue, acted together, and made a common cause in defense of their rights, the artifices of unprincipled and designing men, however deep and well-contrived they might be, would be sure to fail.

It follows then, that the subject on which I have to treat, merits attention in two views; the first, as to the different kinds of government which have existed in different communities in different ages; the second, as to the condition of the society, in the several communities, over which such governments respectively were established. In both branches there are many grades or classes. Government is divisible, from one which is compatible with, and secures to the people under it perfect liberty, to that which subjects them to abject slavery; and society, from a state of entire barbarism, ignorance and depravity, to that of great improvement, intelligence and purity. No proposition according to my judgment, admits of a more satisfactory demonstration, than that in the formation of government, the condition of the society on which it is to operate is to be regarded; that the government which suits one state will not suit another, and that the most improved state of society is that which is best suited to the most free government, if it is not the only one that admits of it. In treating then of government, we must treat of man, for it is for him that the government is formed, and for whom it is indispensable, from the aggregation of a few individuals to that of the most stupendous masses. What then is man? Naturalists give him the highest grade among created beings, and our religion makes his soul immortal. Still he is in a great measure the creature of circumstances. His natural endowments, his passions and principles, are always the same, but these are essentially controlled by moral causes; by the state in which he is, and in consequence in which the society is, of which he is a member. The two branches are therefore intimately connected with, and in the view suggested, inseparable from each other. I will commence with that of government, it being the power which acts on the people, and on which under whatever form, or on whatever principle founded, their happiness must depend. As everything which may be said on this branch must be guided by principle, I will bring to view those, which it is presumed are too well established, to be controverted by any one.

Our system is two-fold, State and National. Each is independent of the other, and sovereign to the extent, and within the limit of specified powers. The preservation of each is necessary to that of the other. Two dangers menace it; disunion and consolidation. Either would be ruinous. It was by the Union that we achieved our independence and liberties, and by it alone can they be maintained. It must therefore be preserved. Consolidation would lead to monarchy and to despotism, which would be equally fatal. That danger must be averted. Both governments rest on the same basis, the sovereignty of the people. Other nations have given us examples of both, of national as well as state, with each of which a comparison of our institutions may be useful, and with which I propose to make it. As however the powers of the National Government originated with the people of each state, and passed from them in the extent to which granted, in their character, as separate and distinct communities, the people of each state form the basis of the system. Consolidation, so far as it has gone, is a diminution of state power, but still the basis in other respects remains unchanged. In looking to either branch, we must look to the source from whence the power emanated, as that is the great feature in our system, in both branches, with the modification given to it in each, which has placed us on more advantageous grounds than was ever held by any other people. In executing this work, therefore, the view which I shall take of the principles of government, and of the state of society, will be equally applicable to both, as well to form a just estimate of the merits of our system, as a fair comparison between it and those of other countries, in both branches.

The view which I shall present in this paper will be elementary, founded on the lights derived from history, and my own observations and reflections, or what I have read and seen through life. In this form and in this stage it is presumed that an illustration may be given, and principles be established, applicable to the whole subject in all its parts, which will be more perspicuous, be better understood, and likewise lessen the labor, than if delayed, until I reach the republics with whose governments and people the comparison will be made.

There are two great principles in government, in direct opposition to each other, on one or other of which, singly and exclusively, or on a compound of both, all governments have been and must be founded. One supposes the sovereignty to be in the people, and in them only. The other that it is in an individual or a few, and that the people have no participation in it, but are the subject matter on which it operates. A third class is compounded of those two principles, partaking in a greater or less degree of the one or the other, and with two or more orders. If in the people, according to our view, it is called a Democracy; if in an individual, a Despotism; and if in a few, Aristocracy. If the government be founded, partly, on each principle, with distinct orders and an hereditary chief at its head, invested with the executive power, we should call it Monarchy. If there be no hereditary chief, and the executive power be vested in an officer elected by the people, we should call it a Republic. This is a generic term, applicable alike to all governments, in which the people hold the sovereignty exclusively, or participate in it, and which are of a mixed character, in which there is no hereditary chief. The ancient authors who have written on the subject of government have made many distinctions which do not accord with the view herein presented. They all had just ideas of the great distinction between liberty and slavery, and of the cause which produced the one or the other state; but in the classification of governments, they seem to have been guided more by the comparative wealth of the parties, and merit or demerit of those who held the office, and exercised its powers, and by the manner in which they were exercised, than as a just regard to principle. Aristotle, one of the most profound writers of that epoch, if not the most profound, on the subject of government, made four species of Democracy;[4] four of Aristocracy;[5] and five of Monarchy;[6] whereas, I can conceive regarding principle, but one of the two first classes, let the government be organized, and its powers be distributed as they may; and but two of the latter, limited and unlimited. He likewise made four species of Oligarchy, which he blended so much with the different grades or classes of Aristocracy, that it is hardly possible to distinguish the one from the other. The basis of both was the rule of a few, but that seems to have been more on the contingencies above stated, than of hereditary right in the parties; Book the 4th, chap.5. The cause to which this vague classification is attributable may, I presume, be easily explained; and in the prosecution of this work, I may endeavor to explain it. I shall simply remark here, that names count for nothing: that principle is everything, and that the great distinction is between a government in which the people rule, and one, in which they are ruled by a power which is absolute. Governments of the latter kind, whatever be their modification, can furnish no example applicable to us. A despot, if a good and wise man, may govern with integrity, humanity and wisdom. A weak and depraved one can do nothing well. The difference reflects honor or disgrace on the individual. It may give to the one exalted fame, for personal merit, and to the other infamy, for his vices and his follies. Such governments, whether the power be in an individual, or a few, turn on different principles from our own, and are subject to consequences corresponding with their principles. The same remark is applicable, in a certain extent, to mixed governments, such as are compounded of the two principles. Where distinct orders exist, an arrangement, by which the people form one, must always have been an affair of compromise, and on their part, of compulsion. Numbers and power being on their side, they could never have consented, voluntarily, to elevate any class above themselves. Compromises in such

---

[4]Aristotle on Politics: Book 4, chap.4.

[5]*Ibid*. Book 4, chap. 7.

[6]*Ibid*. Book 3, chap.10, 11.

cases must have been the result of conflicts, in which each party obtained all that it could, and the preponderance was given to either, according to its good or bad fortune. In the formation of such a government, principle can never have been the ruling object, nor can its example, either in its career or fate, be considered as applicable to us. It may easily be shown that many of the causes which convulsed governments of this mixed character, and finally overthrew them, do not exist here. It is only from governments of the first class, such as were founded on the sovereignty of the people, that incidents which had any influence on their fortune can be cited as strictly applicable to us; nor indeed can they be so considered, unless they were formed in all respects, precisely like our own: and there was likewise a concurrence in every other circumstance to which those incidents were imputable. It is not sufficient that the principle be sound. The government must be sound also, in the organization of its powers, or it will inevitably fail.

It will nevertheless be proper to recur to the three classes of government, to those which are founded on each of the opposite principles, and likewise to those which are mixed, or compounded of both. It is impossible to treat of governments in their most perfect form, or of mixed governments in any form, so as to take a comparative view of their respective merits, without looking at them likewise in their worst state. They all furnish instruction, though it be in different ways, and for opposite purposes. Those in which the sovereignty is vested in an individual, or a few, show an abyss, into which if we fall we are lost. The tendency that way should be guarded against, and to do which it will be useful to see all the avenues which lead to it. Those of a mixed character, which recognize distinct orders, in which opposite and conflicting principles are brought into operation, furnish instruction peculiar to themselves, each class according to its modification. This is the class which stands in competition with our own, and to which of course particular attention is due. Whether a government composed of discordant materials can, under any circumstances, and from any cause whatever, preserve equal harmony in its movement, and promote as effectually the happiness of the people, as one which is homogeneous in all its parts, is the point in contest between them. The organization of those mixed, with the power which each order holds in them, respectively; where deposited, and how exercised, must be looked into. Some of them were better than others. The slightest shade of difference must have been sensibly felt. These differences must, therefore, be shown, and be tested, by the consequences attending them in each.

I have so far treated of the principles on which all governments must be founded, in the outline only. There are incidents to those principles, which form distinctions between the governments founded on each, which it is proper to notice here. These incidents are inseparable from those principles, and may be considered constituent parts thereof. It is necessary, therefore, to trace them in their consequences, to enable us to form a correct idea of the governments founded on each principle, and by means thereof, a fair comparison of their respective merits. The subject must be thoroughly analyzed in all its parts. The government to be compared, and those with which it is to be compared, must be placed respectively in a clear and distinct light, with all their features, with the differences between them, in every, the most minute circumstance, or the comparison cannot lead to a satisfactory result. (There are differences in governments of the same class, as well as in the classes themselves). These differences must also be noticed, since they enter essentially into the character of each government, and form important distinctions between our own and all others that have ever existed.

The terms Sovereignty and Government have generally been considered as synonymous. Most writers on the subject have used them in that sense. To us, however, they convey very different ideas, as they must to all who analyze the subject on principle. The powers may be separated and placed in distinct hands, and it is the faculty of making that separation, which is enjoyed by one class of governments alone, which secures to it many of the advantages which it holds over all others. This separation may take place in the class in which the sovereign power is vested in the people. It cannot in that in which it is vested in an individual, or a few, nor can it in that which is mixed, or compounded of the two principles. This view admits of a clear and simple illustration.

The sovereign power, wherever vested, is the highest in the state, and must always remain so. If vested in an individual or a few, there is no other order in the state. The same may be said of those governments which are founded on the opposite principle. If the people possess the sovereignty, the king and nobility are no more. A king without power is an absurdity. Dethroned kings generally leave the country, as do their descendants. Whatever the sovereign power may perform at one time, it may modify or revoke at another. There is no check in the government to prevent it. In those instances in which it is vested in an individual or a few, the government and the sovereignty are the same. They are both held by the same person or persons. The sovereign constitutes the government, and it is impossible to separate it from him without a revolution. Create a body in such a government with competent authority to make laws, treaties, etc., without reference to the party from whom it was derived, and the government is changed. Such agents must be the instruments of those who appoint them, and their acts be obligatory only after they are seen and approved by their masters, or the government is no more.

In mixed governments in which there are two or more orders, each participating in the sovereignty, the principle is the same. Neither can the king or nobility in such governments create a power, with competent authority, to rule distinct with themselves. In these governments the sovereignty is divided between the orders, and each must take care of its own rights, which the privileged orders cannot do if their powers should be transferred from them. The government is divided between the orders in like manner, each holding the station belonging to it, and performing its appropriate duties. They therefore constitute the government. It follows as a necessary consequence, that the sovereign power and the government even in governments of this class are the same, and that they cannot be separated from each other. It is only in governments in which the people possess the sovereignty that the two powers can be placed in distinct bodies; nor can they in them otherwise than by the institution of a government by compact, to which all the people are parties, and in which those who fill its various departments and offices are made their representatives and servants. In those instances the sovereignty is distinct from the government, because the people who hold the one are distinct from their representatives who hold and perform the duties of the other. One is the power which creates; the other is the subject which is created. One is always the same; the other may be modified at the will of those who made it. Thus the Constitution becomes the paramount law, and every act of the government, and of every department in it, repugnant thereto, void.

It is proper to notice another distinction, not less important, between governments founded on this principle and all others, even those which approach nearest to it. It is only in these governments that defects, which are pointed out by the light of experience, and are sensibly felt, can be amended voluntarily, and with strict regard to principle. When the sovereignty is vested in an individual, or a few, no change can be made without a struggle, nor can any amelioration of the condition of the people be sought otherwise than by petition, nor be granted otherwise than by favor. The sovereign cannot negotiate for a transfer of his powers to another body. The admission of the right in the people to negotiate, would be to admit an equality between the parties, which is incompatible with the principles of the government, and would be sure to subvert it. A change can be wrought only by compulsion, and the necessity of it must be apparent before it will be yielded to. The power must, in fact, be in the hands of those who seek the change, and he or they who hold it be reduced to nothing, before any change can be made. The government will then take such form as those who possess the power may choose to give it; and its late proprietors will likewise experience the fate which the people or their leaders may dictate. The same view is applicable to mixed governments, at least to a certain extent. The power held by the privileged orders, as has already been remarked, was never granted to them by the people as equal parties. It took its origin in a different source, and assumed its shape in any and every stage, as acted on by other causes. To bring the rights of the parties respectively into negotiation, for the purpose of extending the powers of the people, would place them in that respect, essentially in the same relation with each other as in the instances adverted to, and would in all probability have the same result. I speak here of the people moving in a body, under an organization formed specially for the purpose.

In governments of this mixed character, in which the sovereignty and government are united, changes may be made in the same mode by which those orders were established. Such governments always originated with the privileged orders, generally with the prince; never with the people; and were the result of compromises arising from the exertions of the people in favor of their liberties. Changes thus produced, rest on the same ground with the government itself, and will be equally obligatory, while the system is acquiesced in. They must, however, be viewed in the light of the first arrangement, as compulsive on the people, and not as affecting the principles herein laid down.

In governments founded on the sovereignty of the people, in which the two powers are separated from each other, there is a reciprocal action of the government on the people, and of the people on the government, which is unceasing. The people prescribe the rule by compact by which they shall be governed, and in so doing they prescribe the functions and duties of the governing power, which acts on themselves individually and equally. They prescribe also, in the same instrument, the manner in which their own power in the capacity of sovereign shall be exercised. Each party has its duties to perform, on the faithful performance of which the success of the system depends. Precision, therefore, is equally important in both instances. The government must be competent to its objects, and enjoy a freedom of action in the discharge of its duties, within the sphere prescribed, and on the principles of the compact. Misconduct and delinquency in those who administer it should be punishable and be punished, in the mode provided for by the system and executed under it. As the power proceeds from the people, it must be made subservient to their purposes, and this cannot be accomplished, unless those who exercise it feel their responsibility to their constituents in every measure which they adopt, and look to the people and not to themselves. The whole system, therefore, in all its operations, must turn on their suffrages. They must elect those who immediately take their place, and on whom the success of the government essentially depends, and provide for the discharge of their duties. They must elect all who they can elect, and provide for the appointment of all others, by vesting the power in officers who will be responsible to them for their conduct therein in the same manner as for other acts of their official duty. The precise extent to which the election by the people should be carried should be marked with great circumspection and precision. If carried too far, the principles of free government will be violated and the government be overthrown. If carried in any instance beyond the checks of their representatives in the legislative branch, guards should be provided to avert the danger incident to, and inseparable from it, for the more they are drawn beyond that limit the greater will be the danger. The election to that branch should be made as frequent as would be necessary to preserve in full force the powers of the people, but not more so. If too often, the people are always in action and the government loses its force. If too seldom, the people lose their power, which the government gains at their expense and against principle. In making the election, enlarged views should prevail. The community as well as the district should be looked to by every elector.

In the arrangement of the departments of the government, and distribution of their powers, great care should be taken. It must be divided into three branches: legislative, executive and judicial, and each endowed with appropriate powers and made independent of the other. Liberty cannot exist if adequate provision be not made for this great object. The other instances in which the people may exercise their sovereign power relate to the compact itself. If defects are seen in it, they have a right to amend it, and to correct them according to their best judgment, and at pleasure. The regular mode of proceeding is by convention, and which should be invariable in the institution of the government. If in the case of amendments, the agency of the government is admitted in any form, it must be in the mode prescribed by the existing Constitution, and in which it will act merely as the instrument of the people in their character as the sovereign power of the state.

The separation, however, of the sovereignty from the government, when the people possess the sovereignty, depends altogether on their will. They may be united in their hands, in like manner as in the other classes. This is done when the whole people act together and exercise the powers of the government themselves, en masse. This union in their hands, although it differs in certain respects from a like union in those of an individual, or a few, nevertheless produces consequences which are not less important and injurious. It may be shown by an attentive view of the subject, that many of the objections which apply on principle to despotism itself, in its worst form, are equally applicable to this union of the two powers in the people; and that in practice, by the abuses to which it is exposed, and which are inseparable from it, it is often more oppressive.

When it is known that the government of an individual, in which the people have no participation, is despotic, it might be inferred that that which passed to the opposite extreme, in which the whole power was vested in, and exercised by, the people collectively, was the most free and the best that human wisdom could devise. If men were angels, that result would follow, but in that case, there would be no necessity for any government. It is the knowledge that all men have weaknesses, and that many have vices, that makes government necessary; and in adopting one, it is the interest of all that it should be formed in such manner as to protect the rights and promote the happiness of the whole community. The great object is to promote the celestial cause of liberty and humanity; and the perfection of government must consist in its being formed in such a manner as to accomplish this object, by depriving the vicious of the power to do harm, and enlisting not the virtuous only, but all who are not abandoned and outlawed, in support of the government thus instituted. If all enjoy equal rights, merit is rewarded, and punishment inflicted on those only who have committed crimes; the number of discontented and disorderly will be inconsiderable; the great mass will cling to and cherish the government which is strictly their own.

The advocates for governments which recognize distinct orders contend that liberty cannot exist unless the people are held together by a common interest, which must be by restricting them to a limited share in the government, and committing the other portions to distinct hereditary orders. They say that each branch must have a separate interest, and that the power held by the people, and in consequence their liberties, must be exposed to great and unceasing danger, otherwise they will divide into parties, fall under the control of leaders, and become their tools and instruments, to the ruin of the cause. They admit that the portion of power held by the people should be in the legislature; but contend that even in that branch there should be an hereditary check; that the executive should be hereditary, and that the judiciary should be placed beyond their control. In favor of this doctrine they urge that if the sovereignty be vested in the people, under any modification which can be given to the government, there will be but one interest, and in consequence, that the three powers will be concentrated in the ruling authority of the community, which will be the predominating party, and the leader of that party by whom every enormity will be committed and the government be overthrown. They urge particularly, that the chief executive officer should hold his station by hereditary right, and that the people should have no agency in the election or appointment, since, if they have, as there will be many candidates, and each have his partisans, who will embark with great zeal in his support, they will become by excitement, personal interest, and other causes, so identified with their favorite, that the person elected will be opposed on the one side, and supported by the other, without regard to principle or policy.

It will be easy to show that this view is not only erroneous, but that the very facts, which are relied on in support of it prove directly the reverse. The view is founded on the fate of the ancient republics, all of which failed, and on the comparative duration of those which were democratical, with those which recognized distinct orders, the latter of which were more permanent. Why did the democratical governments fail, and why was their existence so transitory? It was because the government was united with the sovereignty in the people, and all the powers, in consequence, concentrated in one body. Why were those of distinct orders more permanent? It was because the powers of the government were separated from each other. In the one class, their concentration was inevitable. It was formed by the government itself, and owing to the then state of the science, and other causes which will be explained hereafter, irremediable. In the other, they were separated by a cause equally powerful, the existence of hereditary orders, and in consequence, likewise, by the government itself. Each order took a portion of the power from the people, and in the degree confined them to one branch only, the legislative, that which they could best execute. If then the separation of the powers of the government by hereditary orders, under all the disadvantages incident to that class; of distinct rights, with the degradation of the body of the people and discordant interest, could secure to those governments a longer existence, does it not furnish ample proof that if separated under more favorable circumstances, the government would be permanent? Will it be contended, that the people cannot be kept together by any other interest than fear? That the enemy must be in the field, in sight, and they be menaced by the bayonet, otherwise, they will divide into parties, yield to their passions, and destroy themselves? If the concentration of the powers of the government, with the sovereignty in the people, subverted the ancient Democracies, as it certainly did, and that fatal cause be removed, and every other precaution which experience has suggested be adopted, how can the system be overthrown? Where are the dangers which menace it? Liberty has its charms and its blessings, in the one case, as well as in the other. The interest of the whole people to unite in its preservation is the same. Can it be believed if they would contend for liberty under the greatest disadvantages; expose their lives, and millions of them perish in the contest, that, when it was placed secure in their own hands, under the wisest organization, that human wisdom, aided by experience, could devise, they would by their vices and their follies break down those strong barriers, and destroy it?

Every danger, however, to which a government founded on the sovereignty of the people is exposed, should be looked at, and guarded against, by all the precautions which human wisdom, aided by experience, can suggest. Man should be viewed in his true character; his virtues and defects should be duly estimated, and the organization be such as to call into activity and give full force to the former, and to suppress the latter.

These two great principles must, therefore, be considered fundamental and invariable, in regard to government, in which the people hold the sovereignty—first, that the government be separated from the sovereignty; the second, that it be divided into three separate branches, legislative, executive and judicial, and that each be endowed with its appropriate powers, and be made independent of the others. It is by a faithful observance of these principles, and a wise execution of them, that tyranny may be prevented; the government be made efficient for all its purposes; and the power of the people be preserved over it, in all its operations. Unite the government with the sovereignty, although it be in the people, and every species of abuse, with the certain overthrow of both, will follow. Concentrate all power in one body, although it be representative, and the result, if not so prompt, will, nevertheless, be equally fatal.

The duties of a government designate the powers necessary to execute them, and the nature of these powers points out the departments in which they ought to be vested with the organizations and number of persons best qualified to execute them. The organization of every free government must be adapted to the duties it has to perform; and the government will be most free in which the organization is most perfect, and the best security provided for the strict observance of the rules prescribed. The prominent duties of a government consist in the enactment of laws, in pronouncing judgment on those laws, and in the execution of them. There are other duties of the highest importance which require the unceasing attention of the government, such as the appointment to office under the government, the intercourse and transactions with foreign powers, in peace and war; the supervision and control of the administration in all its departments, civil and military, in every situation in which the country can be placed. Those of the first two classes belong to the legislature and judiciary. The others fall within the scope of the executive, for it is by it alone, under certain guards, which will have a good effect, that they can be executed with advantage.

The legislature forms the basis of the system. It is the branch to which it belongs to give the best prop to the government, and the greatest support to the liberties of the people, or which by its failure in these respects becomes the principal cause of their overthrow. Its duties connect it, in all its measures, immediately with the whole population of the state, and with the whole territory. The objects of legislation, in the protection of the rights of persons and property, in the imposition of burdens, to promote the welfare and sustain the character of the state in its foreign and domestic concerns, require enlarged views, as well as an upright and legal policy. The legislature of every free state should be divided into two branches, and the number placed in each be regulated by principle, so as to enable it most effectually to accomplish the object intended by it. One should be more numerous than the other, to carry the represention more completely home to the body of the people. The other should be so formed as to be able, by a more calm deliberation, to correct any error arising from a hasty decision of the popular branch. To both there is an obvious limit. I am satisfied that an assembly consisting of four or five hundred members, in its most popular branch, would be sufficiently numerous for the wise management of the affairs of any community, however great its population or extensive its territory; and that the augmentation of it beyond that number could not fail to produce an ill effect. It follows, that the greater the augmentation the worse the effect, by weakening the responsibility of the representative and impairing the power of the people until the government be subverted. The other branch should consist of a sufficient number to inspire confidence, but comparatively of a few, and be composed of persons more advanced in years and of greater experience. The duties of the other branches being altogether different, the number placed in each must correspond therewith. As the judiciary is restricted to an exposition of the constitution and the laws, in cases brought before it, it is manifest that the corps should consist of a few members only. Extend it beyond that number, and it becomes a multitude, incapable of calm deliberation and pronouncing a wise decision. A still greater limitation is necessary for the executive, and for a like reason, a due regard to its duties. It is equally the dictate of reason and experience, according to my judgment, that it be committed to one.

The reasons in favor of committing the executive department to an individual appear to be conclusive. Increase the number to five, or even to three, and the corps will be less efficient in the discharge of its duties, and less responsible to the people. If there be more than one, experience shows that there will be a rivalship between them, and intrigues carried on by each, with the members of the legislature, and through them, with the people, which will produce the worst effect. The same practice will be extended to the departments under the government, which will weaken the administration. The responsibility will also be impaired, because as the numbers would make parties in their favor, throughout the nation, the people would take sides with their respective favorites, and thus the necessary inquiries into misconduct would be checked, and punishment for it often prevented. The members would likewise be elected from different parts of the community, on the representative principle, whereby that tendency would be much promoted, as each section would take an interest in favor of the member sent from that quarter. By committing the power to a single individual, these evils may be averted, and as is believed, without any increased danger to the country. Standing alone, his decision would in all cases be conclusive, and the ministers under him be compelled promptly to obey his orders. There would, therefore, be more energy in the government. His responsibility would also be increased, since the sectional feeling, even in his own quarter, would be diminished, and there would be none elsewhere. By standing alone also, the suspicion of his abuse of power would be much increased, and in consequence his conduct more closely watched, whereby it might be prevented, and if committed, be more easily detected and punished.

As to the mode of securing complete responsibility in this officer to the people, and the faithful discharge of his duties, none can be devised so effectual as by committing the right of impeachment to the popular branch of the legislature, and of trial to the other. The legislature is by far the most numerous; the election of its members is more frequent; they come from every part of the country, and are absent from their constituents a short term only. It is the branch which stands nearest to the people, and is more immediately identified with them; their duties are also of a nature corresponding more with those which the people could perform, if they exercised the government themselves en masse. It is that branch, a misconduct in any of whose members should be punishable by the loss of confidence and non-election only. In every view, therefore, it is the branch on which the people must depend, principally, for their safety, and to which they must commit all those powers in regard to the supervision of the conduct of those in the other departments which they cannot execute, as the sovereign power, directly themselves. To suffer the punishment for misconduct in the chief executive magistrate to rest on the loss of confidence, and non-election by the people only, would neither suit the nature of the office, nor a violation of many of its important powers. The force of the country being in his hands; the intercourse with foreign powers; the supervision and control of the administration, in all its departments, in peace and war; with the appointment to office, and the patronage incident to it; misconduct in many ways might endanger the system, and would evince a perfidy, which would require the severest punishment. Even neglect or idleness, distinctly proved, to the public injury, should not escape notice or censure. The legislature is the only branch within the pale of the system which can exercise this power with effect. Being present, and a party in the government, and in some views, a rival one, the deposit of the power with it will in itself form a great check on misconduct in the other. In this mode, the machine will be kept in motion by its own powers, and on a proper balance. If the power should be taken from the legislature, and vested elsewhere, a new feature would be introduced into the government which would weaken it in all its parts, and might disorganize it. It could not be committed, with propriety, to the judiciary, for that would connect it with the political movement, and the parties which may occasionally be formed by it, which would be incompatible with its duties. A new branch could not be instituted for the purpose, without making the system more complicated, and exposing it to a like danger. The right of impeachment and of trial by the legislature is the main spring of the great machine of government. It is the pivot on which it turns. If preserved in full vigor, and exercised with perfect integrity, every branch will perform its duty, and the people be left to the performance of theirs, in the most simple form, and with complete effect, as the sovereign power of the state. It is not believed that this right could be abused by the legislature. An attack on the executive would draw the public attention to it, and if unfounded, rather benefit, than injure the individual. The whole proceeding would be before the public, in the case of trial, and if innocent, the sympathies of the people would be excited in his favor.

It is indispensable that the three branches be made independent of, and a check on each other. By vesting in the legislature the right to impeach and try the chief executive officer and the members of the judiciary for misconduct, this object will be fully accomplished, as to that branch. Even without this resource, the legislature is less exposed to encroachments from the other branches, than they from it. If the executive should transcend its powers, by acts not authorized by the Constitution or a law, the breach would be so palpable, that it would be immediately discovered, and the incumbent be called to account and punished for it. For the judiciary to make encroachments on either of the branches seems to be impossible, the nature of its powers and duties being so different and obvious. The object most difficult to be provided for, is to arm these two branches with the means of preventing encroachment on them by the legislature; and none occur, which it is thought are so competent, and free from objection, as to invest the executive with the right to negative acts of the legislature, and the judiciary with that to declare a law, which it should deem unconstitutional, void. By vesting these branches with these powers no injury could result, and much benefit might, in many ways. If the right in the executive to negative acts be qualified, as it might be, it would bring the subject again before the legislature, with new light thrown on it, and secure to it a more deliberate consideration. The division between the two branches would draw the attention of the people to the subject, and should the act pass, and be exposed to the objections made to it by the executive, the judiciary, if repugnant to the Constitution, might declare it void; or if consistent with the Constitution, and the power in itself be objectionable, the people might correct the evil, by an amendment of the Constitution. If objectionable on other ground, the people might furnish a remedy, by the declaration of their sentiments respecting it, which might be done in different ways, and with effect. Instances might occur in the progress of affairs, of a political nature, in which the better opportunity enjoyed by the executive to acquire full information, might enable it to negative a bill with advantage to the country. The exercise of the proposed power by the judiciary, could never involve the question of conflicting rights between it and the legislatue, in the character of encroachment on those of the latter. In exercising that power, the judiciary could be viewed only as a tribunal of the people, invested with it, to prevent encroachments, tending to subvert the Constitution, and with it, their rights and liberties.

The legislature and the executive are the branches from which the greatest danger to free government may be apprehended. The union of the government with the sovereignty, and the concentration of all power in one body, is that to which such governments are exposed by the former, and usurpation by the latter. Against usurpation and the monopoly of all power by the legislature, a sufficient guard is provided by the power vested in the executive and judiciary. The danger arises from other causes—the possibility of a tendency to the opposite extreme. If the members of the legislature lose sight of the nation, and look to their sections only, the system is in the utmost danger. Combinations will be formed in support of local interests by means whereof those of a general character will be sacrificed, to the injury of every part, including those who commenced the opposition. At the head of each combination will be found a leader, who will push its cause to an extreme, for his own advancement, at the expense of the public good. A national policy must be cherished and prevail. If the people possess virtue, intelligence, and are devoted to self-government, this danger can never assume a serious form.

In governments in which the sovereignty is vested in the people, and the government is separated from it, a very extraordinary effect is produced. The government which is the instrument, and inferior, operates on those who hold the sovereignty, and in consequence, on the superior. But it operates on the people individually, and not collectively, and as citizens, not as subjects. The government is the agent which executes the compact between the citizens. In governments in which the sovereignty is in an individual, he stands above the law, and cannot be affected by it. His will forms the law by which all others are governed. The government is his instrument, and for others, not for him. In mixed governments, in which there is an hereditary chief holding a portion of the sovereign power, he likewise is above the law, and is not amenable to it. He can do no wrong.

When the government is thus separated from the sovereignty, the people can exercise the sovereign power in the two modes above specified only. One by the election, in the mode and in the extent prescribed by the Constitution; the other by the election of representatives, to serve them in convention for special purposes. In each instance the object is different. In the one, it is to give effect to the government and preserve it, in its course, according to the compact. In the other, it is to act on the government itself, by amendment or otherwise. The people cannot go beyond that limit, in either instance, without taking the government into their own hands, and overthrowing the existing one. If they act directly on those in office, to punish them, for example, for offenses, whether it be by popular movement, or in convention, the government is at an end. To make the government competent to its objects, its powers must be commensurate, under proper guards, with those of the sovereignty, and to preserve the sovereignty in the people, the means of restraining each department within the limits prescribed to it by the Constitution; of enforcing a faithful execution of the duties enjoined on it, and punishing a violation of them by those in office, must be vested in, and be performed by the government itself. The whole system, as heretofore observed, must turn on the suffrage of the people, and the government so formed, that those in office may find that they can obtain nothing independent of the people, nor from them, nor even escape punishment, otherwise than by a faithful discharge of their duties. If the government be thus formed, it cannot fail to accomplish all the objects intended by it; to fulfill its own duties, and to give complete effect to the sovereignty of the people, within the mild and lenient scale specified. The spirit of the government itself will always produce the happiest effect. Men selected by their fellow-citizens for their virtue and talents will not forget the obligations thereby imposed on them. High and honorable sentiments will prevail and be felt in every department and trust under it; and be infused among the great body of the people.

It has been my object in this sketch of the organization and endowment of governments in which the people hold exclusively the sovereignty, to give an outline only, but so far as I have been able, a distinct one. As I shall have to treat of the subject, when I proceed to make the proposed comparison between our government and those which have been mentioned, and must then do it in detail, I will postpone any further remarks on it, until I reach that stage.

When the character of each of these three classes of government is duly considered, it cannot fail to excite surprise, that more than one, that of the people, in its best form, should ever have existed; that the government of an individual, or a few, should ever have been established. Nor can it fail to excite surprise, that a government should have been formed by compromise between the opposite principles, for if the one be radically wrong, how is it possible that anything should be taken from it to improve that which is radically right? How does the fact correspond with this view? What has been the condition of our globe, as to the governments which have existed in its various parts, from the earliest record of time? First of Asia? Was any free government ever heard of in that quarter? Extend the inquiry to Africa, and what the reply? Carthage exhibits the only example, and that for a short period. I come next to Europe, the third quarter, and what has been its fate? The Republics of Greece and Rome arrest our attention with deep interest. They adorned the ancient world, but have long since passed away. They live only in history, through which medium, compared with other governments, they are the objects of our highest respect and admiration. View Europe in modern times, and what the result? Of the attempts which have been made in different countries to establish governments of the kind in question, and of their fate, I shall only remark here, that they have all failed.

Of democratic governments, by representation in its best form, we have no example in ancient or modern times prior to our revolution. The government of the people, wherever it has existed, has been of the people collectively, or en masse, in its worst form, and in consequence its existence has been transitory. Mixed governments have been more durable, but their reign has been short, compared with that in which the people have had no participation; in which they have been slaves. Despotism has been the prevailing government in all ages throughout the globe, including even that portion of time during which the Republic of Rome held an extensive sway, for her government in the conquered provinces which composed more than four-fifths of her territory was likewise perfectly despotic. The tendency has been invariably to despotism, and in it all the ancient republics terminated. To what cause has it been owing that the best government has heretofore never been established anywhere? That so large a portion of mankind have abandoned their rights, and sunk down voluntarily, or at least, without any manifestation of a desire to prevent it, under the dominion of an individual? Many causes have undoubtedly combined to produce this result. I will point out those which appear to me to have had most weight. To do this, we must go to the origin of society, for to it we must trace that of all government. They commence together. Society cannot exist without government, and the nature of the government must depend on the state of the society.

In entering on this, the second branch of the subject, I might pursue the course of naturalists, and examine man, as a class of animals, from the highest northern to the highest southern habitable regions; from the Arctic to the Antarctic circle, in every latitude, climate and country, in both hemispheres, and note all those circumstances, proceeding from either cause, which are presumed to have any influence on his intellect and on the manners and state of society in each community. All naturalists agree in one sentiment, that whatever differences there may now be found between men in intellect, size, form, color or otherwise, there was but one race;[7] that they had a common origin. This analysis, therefore, however correctly it might be formed, would furnish us no consolation; nothing to exalt our ideas of the human race; and in regard to the object which I have in view, leave me essentially in the state in which I now am. The decision does not turn on the point, whether a Laplander, a Samoide, a Tartar, a Mogul, an Arabian, Chinese, Turk or Persian is capable of self-government. It is admitted that the capacity for it depends on the state of society, and as those societies never had such government among them, or made an attempt to establish one, or showed any disposition to do so, it may fairly be conceded, that, be the cause what it may, they are incapable of such government. The scale, therefore, within which the inquiry must be confined, is a very limited one. Among the ancients it includes the Republics of Greece, Carthage and Rome; and among the moderns, the Government of Great Britain furnishes the most striking example.

Such is the nature of man, of the best class of the human race, that so soon as a society is formed, a government must be established over it. Such are his wants, his passions, his principles, and his faculties, and such the elevation and depression of which he is susceptible, that without such government there can be no order or safety in society. So well known is this fact, that if two men were to meet in a wilderness, beyond the reach of law, and the protection of any government, who were strangers to each

---

[7]Buffon.

other, whether rude and savage, or civilized, they would each, instinctively, be apprehensive of danger, having no security for his safety but in his own strength, and doubtful of the character and views of the other. If they should remain together, and find from experience, that their apprehension was unfounded, confidence would grow up between them, and a friendly co-operation in their pursuits ensue. If these two should meet others, the apprehension would revive on their part, and be reciprocated, nor would it be removed on either side without like experience. Even while the number should be limited to a few persons, and their pursuits be equally limited, to that of game for example, a leader of the band would be necessary to preserve order within it, and to take the command in case they should meet other collections of a like kind, the encounter with which might be either hostile, or otherwise, according to circumstances.

Governments being then necessary for every society, however small the number of which it may consist, and in whatever state it may be, the question is, how does it originate? Whence does it derive its authority? These propositions must be examined and decided on principle, and with reference to man and to society in the lights which we are taught by reason and experience to view them.

The origin of government has been traced by different writers to four sources; divine right, paternal authority, election and force. I trace it to two only, election and force, and believe that it has originated, sometimes in the one and sometimes in the other, according to the state of the society at the time, and the number of which it was composed. I think that this proposition admits of a clear and satisfactory demonstration. Before, however, I attempt it, it will be useful to take a brief notice of the other sources, especially as it is to them, that the advocates for despotism and hereditary right have traced it. By confining the attention then to these two sources, the subject will be simplified, and it may then be more easily shown to which source, and to what cause or causes, it is imputable in any and every instance.

Divine and paternal right appear to me to rest upon the same basis, although they have not been so understood by the writers who have traced government to these sources. If divine, the claimant or pretender must prove his title by some miracle, or other incontestable evidence, or it must commence with the parent, and beginning with him be subject to all the views applicable to that title. They must either accord, or be in opposition to each other. No advocate of either places them in opposition, and if they accord, it must be by meaning the same thing, under different names. So absurd are both pretensions, that I should not even notice them, if they had not gained such weight, in one of the communities, of whose government I propose to treat, and at a marked epoch, as to form an important feature, in the works of two distinguished and able writers, on the subject of government, and if I did not wish also, in this elementary sketch, to simplify the subject by getting rid of all such absurd doctrines. Those writers have refuted them, more by reference to sacred history, in reply to the author by whom they were advanced, than as evinced by his faculties, his passions, and career through all ages to the will of the Creator, as marked on the character of man. I shall confine my remarks to the latter, and be very concise in the view I take within that limit.

In tracing regal power to the paternal source, we trace it to a single pair, from whom the whole community must have descended, for otherwise the origin could not have been paternal. If this be the source of power, it must have commenced with the human race, and admitting the authenticity of the Mosaic account, with our first parents, and to preserve the succession, have descended in the right line, to the oldest son, from generation to generation, to the present day. If the right ever existed, it must have commenced at that epoch, and still exist, without limitation as to time, generation, population, or its dispersion over the earth. A limitation of the right, in either of those respects, would be subversive of it. To what term confine it? Through how many generations should it pass? To what number of persons, or extent of territory, carry it? How dispose of it after those conditions should have been fulfilled? The mere admission that such limitations were prescribed, would be to admit that the right never existed; and if not limited, it would follow, that one man would now be the sovereign or lord of all the inhabitants of our globe, than which nothing can be more absurd.

The objection is equally strong to this source of power, rejecting the Mosaic account of our origin, in a single pair, had there been a hundred or a thousand pair, and each been placed at a distance from the others, in different parts of the earth, to form by their descendants, different communities, to give a like origin to the governments established everywhere. The right must have descended, in like manner, to their lineal successors, and their governments extended over the other branches of their offspring, from generation to generation, and still exist, wherever they might be. The only difference in the two modes would consist in the number of sovereigns first created, and still existing, for there could be no more. In all other circumstances, the cases would respond with each other, and the objections applicable to the one, would be equally so to the other, and equally strong. For the government to be paternal, the origin must be in a single pair, descend in the right line, comprise within it the whole offspring in every branch, and through all time.

If it was the intention of the Creator that the government of this globe should rest on paternal authority, it must have been, either by confining it to the descendants of a single pair, and to subject the whole human race to one ruler, or to have created as many pairs as he intended that there should be monarchs, and to have dispersed them, at the time of their creation, over the earth. And to give effect to this plan, either all inter-mixture of the one with the other must have been prohibited, or the earth have been divided by special limits between the several pairs and their descendants, so that there might be no dispute respecting the title. In either case it would follow, that the human race was not created for the benefit and common happiness of the whole, but of one only, in case there was but one pair, and of a few, if more than one. It would follow also, that it was not intended that the first parents should be monarchs, since they would have no subjects except their immediate offspring, and a few of their descendants, but were created as instruments for the aggrandizement of their lineal descendants, some hundreds of years afterwards, when the societies should have increased, and governments become indispensable.

How does this doctrine correspond with Divine authority, as marked by the character of man, or by any other indications by which it may be traced? Cain murdered his brother Abel. Would the commission of that crime have deprived him of the succession? By what authority could this have been done? Could Adam have disinherited him? There existed then no tribunal to decide the question, and had there been such the existence of the power, either in Adam, or such tribunal, would have been subversive of the right. Supposing the government to have descended to Cain, what a strange spectacle would thus have been exhibited, that of a murderer of his own, and then, only brother, inheriting the government, and trans-mitting it to his descendants? How inconsistent with the character, as well as the history of that epoch? Adam inflicted no punishment on Cain, nor did he claim the right to do it. The punishment which he suffered was inflicted, according to the Mosaic account, by divine authority. A curse was pronounced against him, and a mark set on him, whereby he was degraded below, and separated from the rest of the human race. These facts are not calculated to prove that it was intended by the Divine Author of our existence that Adam should be a monarch, or that the right of governing the human race, or any portion of it, should descend to his oldest son.

Do any of the sovereigns of the present day trace their title to Adam, or to any other first parent, or would they be willing to rest it on that ground? We know that they would not, and if they did, that it would fail, since the commencement of all the existing dynasties may be traced to other sources; to causes, such as operated at the moment of their elevation, and varied in different countries. Does any community of Europe, or elsewhere, trace its origin to a single pair, unless it be to our first parents, and which is common to the human race? We know that except in their instance, and at the creation of mankind, societies have never commenced in that form, and that such have been the revolutions in every part of the globe, that no existing race or community can trace its connection in a direct line with Adam, Noah, or others of that early epoch. In the infant state of every society individuals seek each other for safety and comfort. Those who are born together, no matter from whence their parents came, live together, and thus increase and multiply, until the means of subsistence become scanty. A portion then withdraws to some other quarter where those means can be procured, and thus new societies have been formed, and the human race spread over the earth, through all its habitable regions.

Paternal authority has its rights and duties, and is common to every class of animals. It is derived from nature, and has its extents and limits. It is seen in the lion, the tiger, the fish and the bird, as well as in man. It is *parental*, common to the *mother* as well as to the *father*, and binding for a certain term only. As soon as the infant attains maturity, it ceases. It does not extend in any form to the second race, because their parents intervene, and occupy the ground in regard to them which was held by the first over their offspring. If the whole population of any tribe consisted of the descendants of one male and female, all would be equally free in succession, after attaining maturity. No one individual among them would have a right to govern the other. If the parental authority extended in the right line, for example, to the male descendants of one ancestor, it would extend on the same principle, to those of every other, and thus there would be formed by it as many governments within the same limits, and over the same territory, as there were parties to the first association, or rather, there would be no government at all.

From every view that can be taken of the subject, reasoning on principle, the doctrine of divine or paternal right, as the foundation of a claim, in any one, to the sovereign power of the state, or to any power in it, is utterly absurd. It belonged to the dark ages, and was characteristic of the superstition and idolatry which prevailed in them. All men are by nature equally free. Their Creator made them so, and the inequalities which have grown up among them, and the governments which have been established over them, founded on other principles, have proceeded from other causes, by which their natural rights have been subverted. We must trace government, then, to other sources, and in doing this, view things as they are, and not indulge in superstitious, visionary and fanciful speculations.

The remaining sources from which the power may be derived are election and force, and it is from one or other of these, that it always has been, and always will be, derived, for there is none other. The nature of the government, and the manner of its origin, whether attributable to the one or the other cause, must depend on the state of the society at the time it originated, and of which there are two in direct opposition to each other; the one unlettered, rude and savage, the other civilized; and the distance between them, from the most rude to the point to which civilization may be carried, is immense. In the first state, man approaches nearly to the brute creation. He lives, like other animals, on the natural fruits of the earth, and being carnivorous, kills and feeds on them. In the second, he is capable of a very high degree of elevation. Agriculture, commerce, navigation and the arts engage his attention and give him support. A vast range of science is opened to and explained by him. His mind embraces objects, and receives an expansion, unknown to the other state. Government is indispensable in every stage, and becomes more imperiously so in the progress from the one to the other, from the rude to the civilized, according to the degree to which civilization is carried.

I will examine the institution of government in both these states, with the incidents attending it, in each. When formed in a rude state, the remarks which are applicable to one community are in a general view equally so to all. In such a state there is little variety between different communities in reference to the object in question. All unlettered and savage societies resemble each other, and the causes which produce government in each, and the manner of its creation and its form are likewise similar. When formed in a state of civilization, difference may take place between them regarding the advance therein made, and other causes incident thereto, which will produce a corresponding effect. In this state they must be formed, either by a change of the existing government (there having been one from the origin of the society), or by the formation of a new and distinct society, by emigration of a portion of the numbers thereof to a new position, and the institution of a new government over them at that position. As all original societies with whose origin we have any knowledge, both of the ancient and modern world, commenced in the rude state in which state governments were formed over them, and as all the changes in those governments arose from the changes in those societies by their progress from the one to the other state, I will begin with the rude state, and describe according to my best judgment, the government of which it is susceptible, and of necessity adopts. I will then proceed to notice the progress of such societies in civilization, with their capacity to institute a new government better adapted to the state in which they may be, and to maintain such government of these societies, which are formed by migration from civilized communities, and of the governments of which they are capable, I shall take a distinct view in the proper place.

When we speak of man in a state of nature, we contemplate him as rude, unlettered, and unrestrained. In this state he is free and at liberty to do what he pleases. In that state few are seen. Man is by nature a sociable being, and pursuing the impulse derived from nature, clings to his fellow-man. As soon as such numbers are collected, no matter from whence they come, or how thrown together, as to merit the name, a society is formed, and over it such government as they are capable of forming. In this state the government must be of the most simple form, and with very limited powers; it must be that of an individual, or of a few, rather than of laws; and its powers must be confined to the causes which produced it, and principally to the protection of the virtuous against the vicious, of the weak against the strong. When the government is formed as it were, by nature, unaided by science or experience of any kind, it would be impossible for the parties to look profoundly into principles, or to devise the means of preserving them. The provisions of such governments can extend to nothing which those who form them do not understand. All societies in this state must stand on the same ground. It may be shown that this influence is not only justified by experience and reason, but is confirmed by the authority of the most enlightened authors who have treated of the subject.

We have examples in our neighborhood of governments instituted by a people in the rude state, the aborigines of the country, which correspond with those above described. In many instances the power in those tribes is committed to an individual, and in others to a few, who are called elders, and who exercise it in the spirit and extent above stated. Unlettered, they have no written laws, and holding their lands in common, and living principally on game, those which they have are confined to a few objects, such as nature dictates, and are traditional. The cabins which they inhabit, the fruits of their industry, raised on the lands contiguous thereto, and the game which they kill, are their own; and their laws in relation to property extend no further. In respect to wrongs, the code is equally simple. No man is allowed to kill another, because murder is a crime which revolts the feeling of the whole community, and in an exemplary punishment for which they all agree. No reasoning or refinement is necessary to prove it. As these people are free and high-minded, the governments instituted by them may be considered as fair specimens of all governments which have been or may be instituted by a people in a like state.

The progress of these tribes in civilization has been slow, and is yet inconsiderable, even with those most advanced. It is believed that the establishment of schools among them for the education of the youth of both sexes, is the most practicable mode that can be adopted for their civilization; and that by the continuance of such schools, through several successive generations, the object might be accomplished. It is by acting on the infant state only, that civilization can be introduced among them. The aged are beyond its reach. This object it is presumed, might be aided by the institution of a government for them, to be committed in part to our citizens, and in part to their people, by means whereof they might be instructed, gradually, in the science of government, and trained to the exercise of its powers on a more enlarged scale, and on just principles. This, it is presumed, by the influence which we enjoy over all the tribes near us, might be done, with their consent. Whether they will ever be civilized without some such effort on our part is uncertain. Many tribes known to the first emigrants have become extinct, and there is good cause to apprehend, if they remain in their present savage state, that all of them will be. Whether it is our interest to civilize them, or we are bound by the obligations of humanity to do it, are questions which merit the most serious consideration. In their present state they are utterly incompetent to the discharge of the duties of a well organized, free, representative government. Establish such an one over them, and leave the execution of its duties to themselves, and it will soon fail. This remark is applicable to all people in the same state.

If we trace the origin of government to election in this early stage, it must be understood that the persons collected together finding a government necessary, consented that its powers should be exercised by such a person or persons, rather than that the election was made in any regular form, or by the limitation of power, or of the term of service, in the sense in which it is now practiced. If we trace it to force, it may be inferred that crimes being committed or apprehended, and the safety of the society requiring that provision should be made against them by the punishment of the offenders,[8] resistance being made by the worst class, a contest ensued, which terminated in favor of the best, whereby the power was placed in the hands of one or more, who took the lead on the right side. By this view of the origin of power or government over society in such a state, election and force mean essentially the same thing. None would be instituted, if the necessity was not imperative, and in such a state none could be instituted in any regular form, or other than of the most imperfect kind.

Governments thus instituted, however defective in form, or great the power committed to those placed in them, must be free in their origin.

---

[8]Diodorus Siculus, Vol. I. page 19.

The natives being in all other respects equally rude, unlettered, and without property by accumulation, so as to form distinctions between them, as is done in the progress of civilization, the ruler, if there be one, is rather the instrument of the society, than that the members of it are his slaves. They hunt together, prince and subject, if the distinction is admissible; live alike in cabins; and feed on the same fare. Those in power are generally persons of advanced age, and chosen for their good qualities and merit. If one, he is called father, and respected as such; and to this source, it is presumed that the doctrine of paternal power is to be traced. When crimes are committed which require punishment, and the cries of the injured and their connections are heard, the eyes of all are fixed on him, and in consequence he takes the seat of justice, which is that of distinction, and performs the duties of the station. The decision which he pronounces accords with that of all the good members of the society, who constitute always the great majority, and is supported by them. From that seat he then retires to the same simple state of equality with the other members which he held before.

It is in the progress of societies that the relation between the parties changes. The persons thus chosen, generally hold their power through life, and often transmit it to their descendants. The election having had no limitation as to time, and the necessity for the office increasing with the population, to dismiss the aged incumbent and put another in his place, especially if he had given satisfaction, would be an act of injustice which all would disapprove. The possession of the power by the first incumbent for many years, if he had discharged its duties with fidelity, would naturally excite in his favor, and in that of his family, the feeling of the whole community, or at least, of the best portion of it, and hence on his demise, his oldest son would be a fair competitor for the vacant station. Should he succeed, the claim to hereditary right would grow up, which would be sure to beget opposition to it. From this period the ranks in society would be divided. A struggle would commence between those who were friends of self-government and of liberty, and those who preferred a government founded on opposite principles. Sometimes one party might prevail, and sometimes the other. The success of either would take all power with it. If the hereditary claimant succeeded (there having been no division of power into legislative, executive and judicial), the whole would centre in him. If the people succeeded, the whole would vest in them collectively, or en masse. In this state there could be no improvement of the government by the institution of the representative system, or by the delegation of power in any form. The state of the science would not permit it, and besides, the people would always be in a state of alarm, and on the watch, afraid of every one and of every thing. The struggle would thus go on, and under circumstances the most unfavorable to the cause of liberty.

The progress of societies in the rude unlettered state has a strong tendency to augment the power of the chief, and to lessen that of the people. As the population increases, the pursuits of the members become more diversified. Some take to agriculture, others to navigation, commerce,and the arts, while many still hunt the game. The duties of the chief become proportionally more extended and various. The people are also put at a greater distance from him, and each party is less acquainted with the other. His agency would in consequence, in the cases in which he might be called on to act, proceed more directly from himself, and thus he would gradually imbibe the doctrine, especially a chief of the second race, that the power belonged to him, and not to them. If contests should take place, and the people succeed, the effect would only be to transfer the government from one chief to another. Their incompetency to govern themselves, en masse, would be increased with the increase of population, the diversity of their pursuits, and more dispersed situation. The same causes would call for a more efficient government, which they would be equally incompetent to organize, even should the power be in their hands, in any well-digested form, such as should preserve order in society, and secure to themselves the enjoyment of their liberties. With the pursuits of industry a corresponding change would likewise take place in the habits and manners of the people. The two great classes of rich and poor would grow up in each society, which would move in separate bodies, and in opposition to each other. As the latter would form the great majority, it would follow, should the government fall into the hands of the people, that that class would have the complete control. Hence the rich, dreading its consequences, would be apt to incline to the side of the chief or prince.

In such a state of society it would be hardly possible, even should the prince be entirely put aside, for the other parties to institute any regular government for themselves. The state of the science then existing in the world, would, in all probability, still render such an institution impractible, for the wisest heads among them. For an unlettered community, divided into parties different in their circumstances, and in a state of variance and hostility with each other, to accomplish it would be altogether impossible. Should a government be instituted for them by any virtuous and enlightened member of the community to whom they might appeal, organize it as he might, its fate might easily be anticipated. If he should vest the power in the hands of the rich only, it would soon be overset. If in the hands of the people, en masse, under any modification which he might give to it, it might sustain itself longer, but could not be permanent.

The period now adverted to is a very marked one in the history of societies and of man. It is one in which the rude state is essentially abandoned, and considerable progress made in civilization, and in the arts of civilized life. The mass in each society is devoted to liberty, but unable to maintain it. Distinct interests have arisen, by which separate classes have been formed in each community, which are often at variance with each other. While tyrants rule in some, the rich have gained the ascendency in others, and the numerous class of poor retain it in others. Under such circumstances changes would be frequent. Tyrants would occasionally be deposed, and again recover their power. Contests between the rich and the poor would be unceasing, and whenever the latter wrested the government completely from the hands of the former, the power would be sure to pass to leaders who would be apt to quarrel with, and to cut each other off, and thus it would be lost. In this state of civil discord compromises would be apt to take place between the contending parties, which although not formed by regular compact, would have like effect by the acquiescence of the parties. Sometimes the arrangement would come from the prince, who, seeking to retain his power, and knowing that it could not be done unless he tranquillized the state by admitting both the other classes to a participation in the government, he would make an arrangement to that effect. Sometimes it might be the result of conflicts which the exhausted parties could not renew. Such an arrangement could never proceed from the people by accord, as equal parties. In this manner distinct orders would be introduced into the government.

In such a society, in which each extreme, the government of an individual and of the people, under any modification which they could form, being found to be impracticable, and the rich having acquired a force not to be disregarded, it would be natural that experiments should be made of governments of this mixed class, through the whole range between perfect democracy and despotism, that the power of the people should prevail in one, that of the prince in another, and of the aristocracy in others. Although these governments of the mixed character would originate in strife, and take the form which casual events might give them; and although the principle of discord is deeply engrafted in them, and unceasingly felt in their operation, yet they have been more durable than any of the ancient democracies. The tendency however of all governments of this mixed character has been to despotism. When the power of the prince is sustained, if wars ensue with neighboring nations, conquests are made, and new conquests are made, and new dominions acquired, such result becomes almost inevitable. The people remaining in the same unlettered state, reduced to subordination and submission, their minds are broken. The government of the conquered territories is by provinces, and each province by creatures of the crown. The people can have no general meeting, nor in any other mode, in their unlettered state, act in concert. The pursuits of industry, in the great mass, tie them to the soil. If any change in favor of liberty is made, it must proceed from a new state of things, and from other causes. The society must be raised from the depressed and degraded state into which it has fallen; knowledge must be diffused among the people, commencing with a few, and extending by degrees to the whole community, and this can be done only by making those pursuits of industry which contribute to the depression instrumental to their elevation. Property must be acquired by agriculture, commerce and the arts, and knowledge with it. The success of a few will excite emulation with others, and inspire the whole community with hope. By degrees the society may thus be raised to the grade to which it is entitled by nature, and acting with moderation and wisdom, may maintain it.

This view of societies, in their origin and progress, may be considered as applicable to all the ancient republics. It may fairly be inferred, therefore, if the view be correct, that the cause of the people never had a fair experiment in those republics, either from the state of society, or under a government by which such experiment could be made. The governments which they were able to institute, or which the science then permitted, failing, the power passed over directly to the opposite extreme. Fortunate were they when they could escape abject slavery, even for a time, under those of a mixed character. How far it might have been practicable for the people who composed those republics to have improved their system, and to have preserved their liberties, had they been left to the operation of internal causes only, is uncertain. It is known that while the issue was depending, they were all overwhelmed by the warlike spirit, the gigantic growth, and overweening ambition of Rome.

I have so far treated of governments established over societies, in the rude and unlettered state, and of the incidents to such governments, while the mass of the people remained in that state. I will now notice such as may be instituted by societies, in a state of civilization, and which may be done either by old and populous communities, or by emigration of a portion of the inhabitants of such communities to a new position, and the establishment of a new government over them, at such position. I will commence with the effort by an old and populous community, to institute a new government over it, and proceed afterwards to take a view of such government as may be established by emigrants from such community.

In contemplating the institution of a government by an old and populous community, the change of the existing government, and the adoption of

32

another more favorable to liberty, is that which I have in view. We will suppose that the society had passed through a process something like that which has been described; that it had its origin in the rude state, at which period the people were equal and free, but had submitted to such a government as they were, in that state, competent to; that they had had, in their progress, struggles for liberty, and experienced changes of various kinds, until, by the increase of population, and other causes adverted to, they had finally been reduced under despotism. We will suppose also, that they had remained for centuries in that state, until by the extension of commerce, improvement in agriculture, and in the arts and sciences, a new era had arrived; that the mass of the people had become more intelligent; that many among them had acquired great wealth and consideration by their manners, talents and services, which had exalted them by the just standard of merit above any in the privileged orders. A change in this state, by the overthrow of the existing despotism, and the establishment of a free government, could be accomplished only by a revolution and by force. Are a people thus circumstanced competent to such a change? Are they capable of surmounting the difficulties which they would have to encounter in the effort, and to maintain the government should they succeed, after its establishment? These questions involve considerations of high importance to the whole human race. They bear, however, in the first instance, more especially on Europe.

That a government founded on the sovereignty of the people with a wise organization and distribution of its powers, is practicable over very extensive dominions and very populous communities, is certain, provided the state of society throws no impediment in its way. What that state must be, to give effect to such a government, has already been fully explained. All that is necessary is that the inhabitants generally be intelligent, that they possess some property, be independent and moral, and that they organize a government by representation into three branches, a legislative, executive and judiciary, under a wise arrangement, and vest in each the powers competent to its objects. If such a people were possessed of the sovereignty, and were left free under such a government to the operation of internal causes only, having the whole force in their hands, if united and competent, how is it possible that they should fail? It happens, however, that all the most distinguished communities of modern Europe, those which are most advanced in civilization and improvement of every kind, are placed under governments of the monarchic character, many of which are despotic. The institution of free governments in those countries could not be wrought without a struggle. Those in power would not voluntarily submit, nor could the government be maintained afterwards, without encountering serious difficulties, arising from foreign, as well as internal causes. I think proper to remark here, that the people of many of the countries of Europe adverted to, occupy, according to my judgment, much more advantageous ground than was held by those of any of the ancient republics. The class called the people is more intelligent, more independent in its circumstances, and respectable in its character. Skilled in the arts, and intelligent in other respects, as many of the inhabitants of the ancient republics were, still there was a limit within which their knowledge was confined, and beyond which the light of modern times has passed. Science in all its branches has been more extensively explored, and more generally spread among the people. The discovery of the compass has opened all parts of the habitable globe to the enterprising and curious. Commerce has taken a much more extensive range, by means whereof those engaged in it have in successive ages acquired a degree of wealth which has placed them, with their merit in other respects, in elevated stations in every community. The discovery of the art of printing has had an effect still more extensive and important. It has diffused knowledge among the mass of the people, and thereby rendered them better acquainted with their rights, and more able to support them. The different classes of society have been brought into greater intercourse and harmony with each other. The spirit of equality is more sensibly felt, and there are in all those countries many of their most enlightened citizens, in the highest ranks in society, who are devoted to free principles. The light of ages has been shed on the subject of government, and improvements made, especially by representation, which were unknown to the ancient world. Such has been the effect produced by the causes, that it is obvious that several of these governments which are held by monarchs have changed their policy, if not their principles, by accommodating their measures to the popular opinion and feeling. What further changes may be made in any of them time will develope. Nothing that has occurred can be considered as decisive against them, or ought to be discouraging, provided that those who take the lead, act with moderation and humanity. Violence and cruelty will be sure to defeat any attempt that may be made.

Two instances have occured in modern Europe, of efforts made by the people of old and populous communities to wrest the government from the privileged orders, and to establish one founded on equal rights. The first took place in England during the reign of the family of Stuart, and commenced in that of Charles the First. The second in France, and commenced near the end of the century. As it is my intention if in my power to extend the comparison of our governments with that of England, and in making which it will be necessary to notice that effort in some detail, as an example of the governments and of the state of society of this epoch, I shall postpone what I have to say on it until I reach that stage. Of the second, of recent date, I was present and an attentive observer of its most difficult conjunctions. As this epoch forms one of the most interesting events of the modern world, some attention is thought to be due to it in this sketch.

I arrived in Paris on the 2nd of August, 1794, a few days after the fall and execution of Robespierre, and I saw the revolutionary government in operation in its subsequent stages; under the convention; under the directory and the two councils; under the consuls; and I was present when it finally terminated under the Emperor. I was anxious to trace to their sources the causes which produced the very extraordinary occurences which marked that great struggle. I was a friend of the French Revolution, not as an enemy of the Bourbons, for as a citizen of the United States, I was always grateful to them for their services in our Revolution, and lamented the extremity to which the cause had been pushed by their execution. I was the friend of that Revolution as the friend of liberty, in which avowed character I was sent to France as the representative of my government and country. I was therefore an interested spectator as to the cause to which I wished success, but respecting those on the theatre, who acted in its support, and whose merit I could judge only by the view which I took of their conduct, I was altogether impartial.

It was a movement instructive to mankind in regard to the dangers incident to an effort, by an old and populous community, which had been long ruled by despotism, to subvert that government and establish a free one. The movement was in truth revolutionary, and under circumstances which put all the passions in motion under the strongest excitement, without any balance in the system, especially in the early stages, which could give it a proper direction. It was impossible that such an effort should be made without encountering the most serious difficulties arising from internal as well as foreign causes. A monarchy so long established and deeply rooted, could not be overthrown without the concurrence of a large majority of the people, and the collection of such a force as would crush all opposition. Nor could its overthrow fail to leave in full activity the most conflicting elements of which a society can be composed. If civil war in its most formidable shape did not ensue; discontent, which would pervade all the adherents of the former government would still exist and show itself in a variety of ways in the progress of the revolution. Foreign wars would be inevitable, for as the governments of all the other great powers were monarchical, it would be natural for those at their head to conclude that if the monarchy of France should be overthrown, a like fate would befall them. Some time would also elapse before a regular government could be established, and in the interim, the popular movement would control everything. All these difficulties occurred, under circumstances which called into activity, and put to the severest trial, all the faculties and resources, mental and physical, of the nation. The whole people moved, as it were, in a body, and gave proofs of a devotion to liberty, of patriotism and gallantry in the field, which were never surpassed by any other nation. It is not my intention to enter into the details of this great struggle. I shall simply make those comments on it, founded on occurrences which passed under my own view; and others that are well authenticated, which belong to the subject on which I treat.

Each government formed an epoch peculiar to itself, and characteristic of the crisis which had occurred. Extraordinary agitation marked its early stages, of which the government under the Convention gave the most signal proofs. That body formed the government, because, by its acts, the public actions were sanctioned; but it was rather as the organ and the instrument of the popular feeling and will under the excitement which prevailed, than a calm and deliberative assembly, acting according to its own judgment. The people might be said, and especially until the fall of Robespierre, to rule, en masse, and under the greatest possible disadvantages. The government was in effect united with the sovereignty in the people, and all power, legislative, executive, and judicial, concentrated in them. The popular sentiment was ascertained, not from a meeting of the whole people of France in one body, for that was impossible, but from movements in different quarters: Paris, Marseilles, Bordeaux, Lyons, and elsewhere, under local excitements, and without deliberation. Of this sentiment, thus proclaimed, the Convention was the instrument, and at its head was a leader who yielded to the worst passions which could animate the breast of an ambitious competitor for power. Two parties were formed in it, at an early period, one of which was called the Mountain, and the other the Plain. The former was distinguished for its violence and cruelty, the latter for its moderation and humanity. Both were friends to liberty and the Revolution, but they differed as to the means of accomplishing it; and it was that difference, combined with other causes, which gave to each the character it held. Jacobin societies were established from the commencement of the Revolution, through France, at the head of which stood that in Paris, and by which the impulse was given to the others. In the early stages those societies promoted with just views the success of the Revolution, but they afterwards became instrumental to the greatest enormities. Between the Mountain party and this society in Paris the most perfect harmony and concert existed, and which extended in consequence to all the other societies. Robespierre became the leader of the Mountain party, and likewise of the Jacobin society in Paris, and by him, or by his instrumentality, the distinguished members of the party of the Plain, and other illustrious friends of the Revolution, were cut off. The extent to which those enormities were carried, by cutting off innocent persons who took no part in the contest, women as well as men, sapped the foundation of the Revolution, and will always be viewed with horror. This atrocious individual was at length overwhelmed, and led to the guillotine, by which he suffered the fate he merited.

On my arrival at Paris at this awful moment, I beheld a state of affairs of which I had before seen no example, nor anything which in the slightest degree resembled it. Our Revolution exhibited a very different spectacle. The movement of the people with us, in every stage, was tranquil, and their confidence in their representatives unlimited. No animosity or rivalry was seen among them. If any had previously existed, it ceased at that great crisis. We had no distinct hereditary order in the community; no hierarchy. We had but one order, that of the people; nor had we any citizen among us who did not rest on his merits and the opinion entertained of it by his fellow-citizens at large. The whole body, therefore, clung together on the purest principles, and the most simple and perfect form. But on the theatre then before me, all the conflicting elements to which I have referred were in full activity, the effect of which was visible on every object which presented itself to view. The adherents of the monarchical government were anxious to overthrow the existing one, and active in promoting that result. The nobility, who had remained behind, were generally of that class, all of whom were degraded, and most of whom had suffered by the Revolution. The hierarchy formed a corps equally numerous and active. Their lands had been wrested from them and sold, or were at market. All these classes acted in concert, but being overwhelmed, moved as it were under the mask. The people contributed their part to this disorderly and frightful spectacle. The Convention was, for the moment, comparatively calm, as was the city, but the tranquillity was of a character to show that the passions which had produced the late storm were rather smothered than extinguished. Other explosions were dreaded, and confidence, even among those who had been most active on each side, seemed to be, in a great measure, withdrawn. The Mountain party still held the majority in the committee which were charged with the executive government, and that party was not entirely crushed in the Convention.

My own situation was the most difficult and painful that I had ever experienced. Our treaty of commerce of 1778 had been set side, and many of our vessels seized and condemned, with their cargoes, in violation of it. Some hundreds of our citizens were then in Paris, and the seaports of France, many of them imprisoned, and all of them treated more like the subjects of their enemies, than the citizens of a friendly and allied power. An hostile attitude was assumed toward our government and country, and war seriously menaced. Of this disposition I felt, personally, the most mortifying effect, my recognition being delayed and likely to be refused. I saw distinctly that no impression could be made on the Committee of Public Safety, and was fearful if I should acquiesce in the delay of my recognition, the ill will toward us which pervaded that body would be extended generally to the Convention, and throughout the nation. On full consideration I was satisfied that the injuries already received would not be redressed, nor greater averted, without making an appeal as it were to the real government, the people, through the nominal one, the Convention, and by means thereof to bring the cause fairly before the nation. I knew their object was liberty, and that they had caught the spirit in our struggle, by the part they had taken in it, many of whom had carried it home, and infused it into the great body of the people. Our eyes are naturally turned to an illustrious individual who lately visited us, who fought and bled in our cause, and whose services in its support can never be too highly appreciated or liberally rewarded. I knew that there stood at the head of our government one, who by his devotion to that cause, and the services he had rendered to it, was entitled to, and held in the highest veneration by the French people; and was persuaded, if I brought before them convincing proofs of his good wishes for their success, supported by that of the other branches of our government, that the hostile spirit which had been manifested towards us by the French Government, would be subdued, and my recognition immediately follow. It was on this principle that I addressed the convention, and with the desired effect, having been received by that body itself on the next day. That such should have been the state of affairs, as to compel me to resort to such an expedient, is in itself a sufficient proof of the disorder in which the Government of France then was, and of the difference between it and all settled governments, whatever be their form.

From this period the power was transferred to the party of the Plain, who held it the residue of the term of the government by the convention. The conduct of this party corresponded with its well-known principles. It looked to the cause, and pushed it forward with zeal and perseverance, and as I thought with perfect integrity. It sustained also its character for moderation and humanity, for I saw in its progress, in the trial of some of the leading members of the Mountain party who had survived, and were denounced before it, a disposition rather to forgive, than avenge the injuries it had received from that party. Several attacks were made on the convention during the rule of this party, by popular movements in Paris, particularly by those of Germinal, Prarial, and Vendemiare, which were met with firmness, and repulsed by the force arrayed on its side. These movements were either excited by foreign powers or by members of the Mountain party. Among the important objects which now engaged the attention of the convention, was the formation of a constitution, in which it succeeded by the institution of the government of the Directory, and the two Councils, to which the power was transferred on the 31st of October, 1795. The proceedings under this government assumed a different character from that which had been acquired by those under the convention. They were more tranquil and orderly, and the government itself, in all its departments, more operative and efficient. The people confined themselves more within the limit of their appropriate duties, as the sovereign power of the state, and left the government more free to perform those which belonged to it, as their representative and responsible organ. The government of the Consuls was a step toward monarchy, in which it terminated in the imperial form.

In the progress of this Revolution I beheld, with great interest and satisfaction, the wonderful effect which it had, from year to year, by the agency of the people in the government on their intelligence and capacity for self-government. I noticed this in my first mission, during my residence in Paris, from 1794 till 1797; and I was more sensibly struck with it on my return to France in 1803. It was by the patriotic zeal and devotion to liberty of the whole French people, that the most gallant exploits were performed that the modern world had witnessed: that all the surrounding nations had been repulsed, and many subdued, so that in truth the Revolution was accomplished when the last change took effect. Satisfied I am, had those who had gained great popularity, by the eminent services which they had rendered, looked to the cause a few years longer, and not to themselves, the Republic might have been saved. The people had much improved in their capacity for self-government, yet their emancipation from the opposite extreme had been too sudden, and the interval too short for them to have become, in all respects, competent to it. They were devoted to the Revolution, and were grateful to those who had signalized themselves in its support, especially by gallant exploits in the field, and by victories over the powerful armies which assailed them. The names of those commanders became identified with the cause, and in their elevation without making the proper discrimination, they looked to its support, rather than to its overthrow, and thus their best propensities, as well as their frailties, were practiced on and made instrumental to that result. In making this remark, I indulge no feeling of personal hostility to Napoleon Bonaparte, in whose favor the change was wrought, and who was the principal actor in it. No one thought more highly than I did of his gallantry in the field, and of his talents as the commander of his army, and personally I had no cause of complaint against him, for in my second mission to France, when he was at the head of the Consular Government, I was treated by him with kindness and attention. I look only to the change, and to the causes which produced it.

An enlightened and virtuous people, who are blessed with liberty, should look with profound attention to every occurrence which furnishes proof of the dangers to which that cause is exposed. The effort was made by a great nation, distinguished for its improvement in civilization and in all the arts of civilized life; advanced to the utmost height in every branch of science that the human intellect has attained, and respected for every useful as well as polished acquirement throughout the civilized world. Having witnessed personally that effort, in the extent that I have stated, I have thought that a brief notice in this place of its progress and fate might have a good effect, and have, therefore, given it.

I will now proceed to notice such societies as may be formed by emigration of a portion of the inhabitants from civilized communities into another country, with the establishment of new governments over them in such country. I shall note some prominent distinctions between governments established by societies in this and the other state, to show the eminent advantages which the latter have over the former, as well in the capacity to institute free governments, as to preserve them.

Of this class, that is by emigration, there may be two of different character. The emigrants may take possession of a new territory, and institute an independent government of their own, such as they prefer, or they may emigrate under the protection and authority of the parent country. Of the first kind, the state of improvement to which the science has been carried is the natural limit of any human institution. Prudent men will be more disposed to adopt institutions under which they have lived, if of the free class, than to make experiments of untried projects, which are suggested by conjecture and fancy only. Governments thus instituted corresponding in their form with those of the parent countries, and the state of society being the same, would be apt to experience a like fate. If the government of the colony is formed by the parent country by charter, its fate will depend on a variety of circumstances, and particularly on the interest which the parent country takes in the emigration, and the connection which it intends to preserve with the colony; on the spirit in which the emigration is made and the causes which produced it; and on the character of the emigrants. If the institution is made in its great features popular, and the power of that branch of the government falls into the hands of enlightened and virtuous emigrants, the control of the colony, during its infant state by the parent country, will form a nursery of the best kind for free principles. Civilized men will take possession of the woods, and the freedom of the hunting state be preserved, without the barbarism incident to that state. The widely separated parties of extreme wealth and poverty will not be known among them. The pressure from the parent country, however slight, will unite them at home, and thus form but one class among them, the whole of which will be united, when the emergency requires it, against oppression and in favor of liberty. The intelligence and correct principles of the parents will descend to their offspring, and thus the society will grow up from its infant state to maturity, instructed in the knowledge, and trained to the support of popular rights and dismemberment, find them in the best state to preserve them. An enlightened community, perfectly free, having the whole power in their hands, with no opposing interest to contend with, may organize the best government that human wisdom can devise, and be sure to preserve it.

CHAPTER II

A COMPARATIVE HISTORICAL VIEW OF THE GOVERNMENT OF THE UNITED STATES AND THE REPUBLICS OF ATHENS, LACEDEMON AND CARTHAGE

THE elementary view above presented of government in its principles, and the incidents to those principles in the different classes of government, and of society in the different states of which it is susceptible, and of its capacity for self-government, regarding the state in which it may be, will aid me in the prosecution of the work in which I am engaged. There is no part of the subject in either branch to which this view will not apply, or in which it is not supported, as is believed, by the well attested history of the human race in all ages, throughout the globe.

The comparison which I propose to make of our government with those of other countries, will be confined, as has already been observed, to those of Greece, Carthage and Rome, among the ancients, and if my health permits of Great Britain among the modern. With those of Greece, I shall confine it to those of Athens and Lacedemon. The first of these was a simple democracy, organized and exercised in the manner known to the ancients. The second was a mixed government with distinct orders. In regard to the first, the principle being the same with that on which our governments are founded, the example of a single government will be sufficient. In the view taken of it the defects of all governments of that class applicable to our own system, must proceed from other causes than the principle; and in treating of the defects of our government, those of all others of the same class may be noticed. When the principle is different, several examples may be necessary, and with that view I shall extend the comparison to the other governments mentioned, which differed from each other in the number of orders and division of power between them. In examining the Government of Athens, I shall have in view that which was instituted by Solon, it being admitted by all to have been the best they ever had, and in effect the best of that class that was known to the ancients. Considering the society and the government connected and identified with

41

each other, as I do, and having an influence each on the other, I shall commence with the origin of both, and trace them, with the great events which marked their career, to the adoption of that institution, and during its existence. In examining the Government of Lacedemon, I shall have in view the Constitution of Lycurgus, and pursue the same course in tracing the origin of the society and government of that people with their progress, that I propose to do with those of Athens. I shall likewise endeavor to do equal justice to those of Carthage and Rome, noting their best epochs, with the causes of their decline and fall.

In regard to the modern world, the government of Great Britain furnishes the most interesting example. In treating of it, the distinctions between it and governments of a like kind among the ancients, and likewise between the societies of those two great and distant epochs, may be noticed.

In a development of the organization and endowment of the Democratical Government of Athens, and of its defects, with the proper remedies for them, a wide range will be opened for the practical illustration of the great principles of the science. There was nothing sound in that government but the principle on which it was founded. A full development therefore of its defects, with the remedies for them, will in those respects, if well executed, leave nothing untouched in relation to governments of that class, and include much which is applicable to the other. It will be found that the principles which apply to the organization and endowment of a government founded on the sovereignty of the people, will embrace all the considerations that are applicable to this class, and many that are equally so to the other; will apply to those which recognize distinct orders, and to all governments in which the people participate, or that have any pretension to liberty. In governments in which the people possess, exclusively, the sovereignty, the people must be protected against themselves, otherwise, such is the nature of man, that oppression, with the overthrow of the government, will be inevitable. The rule of a single body, and of a single man, must be prevented. Contests for power between individuals, if they cannot be controlled, must terminate there, and guards must be provided for the purpose adequate to the end. The door must be closed against ambition, and against selfish views of every kind which, by being yielded to, may operate to the injury of the cause. A fair compensation should be allowed for service, and honorable distinction for exalted merit; but such should be the organization and endowment, as to make the government by the operation of selfish as well as more lofty motives in those in office the instrument of its own preservation, rather than of its subversion. The guards which are deemed necessary for the accomplishment of these objects, have been noticed in the preceding part of this sketch. In the view which I propose to take of the defects of the Athenian Government I shall treat the subject more in detail.

In governments which recognize distinct orders, be the state of society what it may, the people must likewise form the basis of the system. The legislative power must be essentially in their hands, and it must be well organized, or they will soon have none. Place it in an hereditary branch, and there can be no liberty. Give to a prince a larger portion than is prescribed by principle, and strictly executive, and he will soon absorb the whole, or be overthrown. The same remark is applicable to the aristocratic branch, or that of the nobles. Its powers must be limited, and the possibility of encroachment by it on the other branches be prevented, or a like result will follow. The nearer therefore such governments approach to well established principles, both in the organization and endowment of their branches, the more tranquil will their movement be, and the longer their duration. A defect in those respects will operate differently in the different classes, arising from the difference of principle in the government, and of interest in the parties, but an irregular and disorderly movement, with the final overthrow of the government, will be certain in both. I shall endeavor, therefore, in treating of the Government of Athens, to illustrate and establish those principles, and in a manner to admit their application, so far as it may be practicable to both classes of government, with a view to abridge what I should otherwise have to say, when I treat of the governments of the other class, and on the presumption that the illustration thus given will throw light on the subject generally as I advance in the execution of the work.

The same view is applicable to governments which recognize distinct orders with opposite interests contending against each other. The hold which each order has in such governments, the people on their part, and the other order or orders, when there be more than one in theirs, with its nature and extent, the manner in which it has been exerted and the effect produced by it will claim a like attention. The power which the people or either of the other orders held in any given instance, when contending with another, having an opposite interest, would, it is presumed, be exerted in like manner, and produce the same effect in every other instance that it had on that, the circumstances being in all respects equal. When a principle is established as to either class, it will be conclusive as to all like cases of that class, and of the other, so far as it is strictly applicable. The same view will be taken, and of course pursued, in regard to the societies of the several communities, of whose governments I shall treat. Where the state is the same, corresponding effects, under like causes, may be expected in every instance. I shall say nothing more of any government or people than is indispensable to the object I have in view. In this mode I shall abridge essentially the work, as I shall the labor, which I should otherwise be forced to bestow on it.

When a principle is supported by the example of a single government, and that example is strictly applicable in all its circumstances to other governments and people of which I shall treat, I shall make the application without a further illustration of the principle. Principles in government, where the circumstances are in all respects similar, as to order, distribution of its powers, and the state of society, are as invariable and eternal, as in any other science, mathematics, or any branch of experimental philosophy.

In taking a view of the origin and progress of the Athenian and Lacedemonian Governments and communities, for the purposes contemplated, I must look in a certain extent to those of all Greece. Those Republics formed, from the earliest period of which we have any knowledge, two of the principal states of Greece. They took a distinguished part in all the concerns of that people internally, as they likewise did in those which bore on foreign nations. The misfortunes of Greece, as well as her glory, were in an eminent degree attributable to them. Their progress, therefore, was connected with that of the other states, as was their fate, for they were all involved in one common ruin. This view is necessary in making the proposed comparison with the state governments, but in extending it to that of the general government it is indispensable.

Of the confederated system, other people, and particularly those of Greece, have also given us examples, of which, so far as they may merit attention, I shall take notice at the proper time. All such bonds rest on the elements of which they are composed, and in consequence of which the states and people, thus held together, are composed. It is necessary, therefore, to form a just idea, in the first instance, of those elements in all their parts.

There are different modes by which the object I have in view may be accomplished. One by a preliminary digest of a government, in its principle, organization and endowment, which I should consider the most perfect, and to test all the governments above enumerated, including our own, by that standard. Another to make the comparison with the democratical government of Athens, separately, showing its defects, with the remedies for them, and then to show that we have avoided those defects, and attained by our organization and endowment the utmost degree of perfection of which any government is susceptible. This being done, to compare our governments with those of a mixed character, with a view to decide the relative merit of the two classes. A third is, to make the analysis of all the governments above enumerated, in the manner stated, and to give a sketch of the career and fate of each in succession; and then to make the comparison between our governments and each of the others in all the points which they respectively involve, commencing with that of Athens. To the first it might be objected, that the sketch which would be given of the most perfect government would be theoretical only, and that the references which might be made to other governments might be regarded as forced constructions, for the purpose of supporting such theoretical dogma. To this it may be added, that the elementary view above presented goes as far in the establishment of the standard suggested, as we can go, without the aid of example, supported by the career and fortune of the governments referred to. If this view be correct, the organization and endowment of a government corresponding with it are so obvious that they will occur to all who are conversant with the subject. To the second it might be objected, that the view presented would be equally limited and unsatisfactory. The example of the Athenian Government, which had failed, however great and numerous its defects, and well-established by reason and arguments, and supported by its career and fate, might not be deemed sufficient to prove that that was the best class, or that we had attained by the organization and endowments of our governments that standard of perfection to which we aspire. To do justice to the subject, and make a fair comparison between our governments, which are founded on the sovereignty of the people, and those which recognize distinct orders, we must place each class on the best ground on which it can stand, and give to it, also, by the most incontrovertible evidence, all the support which can be adduced in its favor.

On full consideration, I am satisfied that the third mode ought to be preferred. It secures all the advantages which may be derived from either of the others, with many peculiar to itself, and is at the same time free from the objections applicable to each. The comparison must be practical, founded on the experience of each government, and extend to principle, as well as the organization and endowment of each, and likewise to the state of society in each community; and this can be better done by having the whole subject before us at the same time than it detached parts. The ancient republics formed a system peculiar to themselves. Their governments varied from each other, not in principle alone, but in many other important circumstances; still there were analogies between them, even when the principle was different, which were peculiar to that epoch. Our governments differ from them all; from the Athenian, not in principle, but in other circumstances of vital importance. The Government of Athens was founded on the sovereignty of the people, but the power was exercised in a manner to defeat its purposes. The accord in principle was in fact, as will be shown, nominal only, for such were the organization and endowment of that government that it could not fail to be oppressive. The other governments enumerated were of a mixed character, founded partly on one principle, and partly on the other. Their defects, so far as the sovereignty of the people was recognized in them, being of a like character with those of Athens, would of course produce, in what related to the power of the people, a corresponding effect in those governments with that which they produced in the Government of Athens. It follows, therefore, that by keeping them together, and taking a minute view of each, and a combined view of the whole, the defects of each, and of the ancient system generally, may be more distinctly shown, than by detaching them from each other. The connection is such even between those which are simple, or founded exclusively on the sovereignty of the people, and those which are mixed or compounded of the two principles, that the illustration of either cannot fail to throw light on the others. The British Government, although it varies essentially from the ancient republics in the modes in which the power of the people is exercised in it, yet as it recognizes distinct orders, all the objections which apply to them on that ground, apply with equal force to it. It must therefore be placed in that class, noticing with impartiality and candor the distinctions to be taken between them. I shall therefore proceed, in the execution of this work, in the manner stated, commencing with the Government of Athens, proceeding next to that of Lacedemon, and afterwards to the others, in the order in which I have placed them.

The view which will thus be presented of the governments of the ancient republics and that of Great Britain, and likewise of the state of society in each community, will be practical. The cause of the failure of each of those republics may be distinctly seen. There is no material fact relative to the government of either as to its principle, its organization, or the endowment of its branches, with the effect produced thereby, or as to the society of each, involving its capacity for self-government, but what may be clearly proved. The same remark is clearly applicable to the British Government from its origin to the present time. In this mode it is presumed that a correct standard, tested by experience, may be formed of the best government in principle, organization, and endowment, which human wisdom can devise; of that which is most free, and best calculated to preserve liberty; and to maintain order, as it may likewise be of the state of society necessary to give effect to such government. With this standard our system may be compared, and a correct judgment be thereby formed, whether it has attained the utmost degree of perfection of which government is susceptible, or is defective in any branch, and if in any, in what particular circumstance, and what the proper remedy is for such defect. The latter is a great object of the present inquiry. All the moral as well as the physical sciences admit of demonstration, but none with greater certainty than that of government. When the cause and effect are distinctly seen, as may be done in that science by the examples which history furnishes, no mistake can be made by those who are unprejudiced and seek the truth. The demonstration may be considered as complete. In this mode I shall pursue this inquiry, and with that sole object in view.

There are three great epochs in the history of the human race, or rather of that portion of it, whose manners and institutions form the object of this inquiry. The first commenced with the origin of the ancient republics, and terminated with them. The second commenced with the governments which were erected on the ruins of the Roman Empire, and comprises their career to the present time. The third was formed by the discovery of this hemisphere, and the revolution into which it led, with the governments which have been founded on its principles in these states. Each of these epochs is marked by characteristics which are peculiar to itself. Government in each took its origin under the influence of special causes applicable to the epoch. In the first the race of man was limited. The collections were small, and each band or tribe adopted the government which suited it best, or submitted to that which the exigency required and nature dictated. The changes which occurred in the progress of those societies, especially in the early stages, were attributable more to internal than to external causes. These primeval institutions were cherished and maintained by each society, so far as it was able, until they were all subdued and reduced under one which happened to be the most powerful. In the second epoch the earth had become crowded with inhabitants, and that republic which had risen to the greatest height, which had conquered all the others, and a great part of the other known regions of the globe, was now destined to experience the ill fortune which it had inflicted on other states. This nation, which owed its elevation and grandeur to free principles, had abandoned those principles, and by the indulgence of every species of debauchery and vice, sunk down under despotism into a state of the most miserable decrepitude and imbecility. At this period many barbarous nations, incensed at the usurpation and tyranny which had been exercised over them, distant from each other, and without concert, fell on different parts of that vast empire, and overcame it. These nations established in the parts which they respectively conquered, such governments as they thought best calculated to preserve their conquests, and to keep the people whom they had subdued in subjection. These governments were essentially military, a chief at the head of each, with inferior and subaltern officers under him, of different grades, the same, as is presumed, in the first instance, leader and others, who had commanded the invading force and made the conquests. Under such circumstances it would be long before the conquerors and the conquered could be completely incorporated and become one people; and hence the order which was established in the commencement would be preserved. In this manner the governments of modern Europe originated, the strong features of which are still marked on all of them, and especially those most free. The third epoch commenced in a form different from either of the others. The parties to it were of the same European race, but they commenced their career by emigration to the new world. The state of civilization and improvement to which the emigrants had arrived, the causes which produced the emigration, and the spirit with which it was made, with the institutions under which they settled, placed them in their origin on more favorable ground than was ever held by any other people. It is to the governments which have been instituted by the descendants of these emigrants, that we owe the felicity which we now enjoy, and that the present epoch owes its importance.

The writers on the subject of government, ancient and modern, composed their works under the influence of the examples before them, and of the state of society existing at the time. Their works are characteristic of the epochs at which they lived. In the first there were two dangers, that of despotism, and the government of the multitude, both of which were equally menacing, and both of which they viewed with equal horror. In that age society was comparatively in its infant state, and in the governments that were mixed, the orders were not distinctly marked by any well-digested principle. In guarding against one extreme, they were apt to run into the other. It was owing to these causes, that we find the definition given of the several classes of government at that epoch, so vague and indeterminate, so little accordant with principle. In reasoning on man, under the influence of the different classes of government, with the modifications then known, and on all abstract subjects connected with his principles and passions their works are profound, but they are nevertheless confined within that scale. The same remark is applicable to those who lived in the second epoch, which was threatened with a single danger only, that of despotism. It was natural that those writers who lived under governments which extended to the people a portion of liberty only, and which were menaced with despotism, should look to that danger alone, and exert all their faculties to prevent it. It could not be expected that they would look to the abuses and dangers of a system which they put in contrast with that which they dreaded and wished to avoid.

When we are informed that Aristotle had collected the constitutions of one hundred and fifty-eight people, from which he digested his work called

Politics or the Science of Government, we are enabled to form a tolerably correct idea of the number of inhabitants and extent of territory of each state, and likewise of the causes to which the form of those governments was attributable. We see at once that each community must have consisted of the inhabitants of a village, and that its territory could not have extended much beyond it. He treated of free governments, or of such as were so considered by him, and in consequence, of those in which the people held either the entire sovereignty, or a portion of it. His object was, in making this collection, to show the good features and defects of each, and to give his opinion in favor of that which appeared to him the best, with a view to promote the liberty and happiness of mankind. There were then few free governments beyond the limits of Greece. The Carthagenian was one, and of which he spoke in very favorable terms. Of the Government of Rome he said nothing, which proves that the collection consisted almost altogether of the Governments of Greece. That work was lost. His essay on the Science of Government has been preserved. If one-tenth of the number of constitutions said to have been collected by him consisted of those of Grecian states, it would follow that they were of the character above mentioned.

Among the writers of the second epoch, Locke and Sydney of England, and Montesquieu and Rousseau of France, hold a very distinguished rank. The essays of the two former correspond with the remark already made. They lived at a very unsettled period, and looked at one danger only. Those of the two latter are more elementary and general, more in accord and spirit with those of the first epoch, arising as is presumed from the government under which they lived, and the fear of giving offense to those in power. The works of all these writers are very able, and exalt the fame of the authors. They nevertheless do not point out either the advantages or the special dangers of our system, for they did not contemplate it. I may take further notice of them hereafter. My object is to look at the dangers as well as the advantages of our system, and to point out its dangers, so far as I may be able, with the means of averting them. With us there is at present no existing disease. We are on the contrary blessed with perfect health. Our object is to preserve that state, and prevent a disease. It is, therefore, our duty to look to the dangers which threaten liberty, from any and every direction, and to guard against them.

Considering government and society as identified, each depending on the other, it has been my object in this elementary sketch, after fixing the principles of government with their incidents and a brief outline of the best organization and endowment that can be adopted for free governments of every kind, to present the most correct view of both branches of the subject that I have been able, as they have existed in the two preceding epochs. There are two sources from which the most correct information may be obtained of the best organization and endowment of free governments that can be adopted, authentic history and scientific essays on the subject of government itself, compared in both instances by enlightened men. From history we derive a knowledge of wants, from the origin of the communities of which the authors respectively treat, to the period at which their narrative terminates. The state of society and of government, with the changes which occur in each, in the progress of such communities, fall within the scope of this class of writers, but rather as descriptive of the actual state in every stage, than a profound analysis of the subject, in either of its branches, so as to meet the precise objects of this inquiry. It is more the duty of an historian to narrate the transactions of a government in its internal concerns, and those with foreign nations, than to analyze with vigor its parts, and to compare its merits with the governments of other people. It belongs to a writer on government to take a more comprehensive and minute view of the subject on principle, its organization, endowment, and every other circumstance connected with it. If the essay be of that character, and the writer be blessed with great talents, nothing that belongs to it, which was then known, would escape his attention. If he does not treat of the state of society, especially if a writer of the second epoch, it must be because the condition of the people was such that the share in the government for which he contended in their favor, was so limited, as to preclude all discussion on the subject, without an acknowledgment that they were incompetent to the discharge of any of the duties of any regular free government whatever.

I have stated that there are three great epochs in the history of the human race, and that each was marked by characters as to government and society peculiar to itself. I have stated also, that the third, to which we belong, has placed us on different and more advantageous ground, in both respects, and as to the means of supporting free government, than was ever held by any other people. To prove this beyond all doubt, it is necessary to place the governments and societies of each epoch in their true character, and to show the difference between them in every material circumstance. In the view which has already been presented, I have derived all the aid from both the sources alluded to, as to the first two, that I have been able. There is not a fact stated, which is not supported by the best authorities in each, and where they apply, in both. As however the writers on the subject of government draw more distinctly the line between governments of different classes, and in consequence between those of the different epochs, and likewise between the epochs themselves, I have thought that a summary but correct view of the contents of the works of the most distinguished writers of the two preceding epochs, would give a more satisfactory confirmation of the government and state of society in each, and thus enable me to show the difference between ours and both, than could otherwise have been done, and have therefore drawn it. The authors of whose works I shall give such sketch, are considered the ablest that have written on the subject of government. They are so regarded in our schools of instruction, in our literary institutions, and by scientific men generally in the United States and in all free countries. As they do not embrace our system, they could not show its advantages over those which preceded it. On the contrary, the writers of the second epoch, whose works are most read and relied on, have preferred and recommended governments of a different kind. Had our governments been before them in successful experiment, as they have been since their institution, they would, I have no doubt, have recommended them in preference to all others. Having their own, or rather those for which they contended, for there was then nothing settled, and the ancient system only before them, it may fairly be inferred that they concluded that the alternative was between those two; and preferring their own, for their own country, and for obvious reasons, have declared that sentiment in the matter stated. In the study of the science of government, especially by our youth, it is proper that their attention should be drawn to this feature in those works, with the probable cause of it. It is improper that they should adopt an opinion unfavorable to our system, on the sentiment expressed by those writers, which it may fairly be presumed, had they been acquainted with it, they would not have entertained. I have therefore found in this circumstance an additional motive for giving a sketch of their contents.

Among the writers of the first epoch, Aristotle is the most distinguished. Plato composed a work on the subject of government. He drew two projects, but they are so theoretical and objectionable in every view; so little applicable to us, and even to the age in which they were written, that they need not be noticed. Plutarch, in his Lives of Distinguished Men, gives sketches of the governments which were formed in the progress of different communities, from their earliest ages to this time, by the princes or chiefs at the head of each, voluntarily, or by persons to whom the power was committed by the contending parties, which are instructive in that view, as well as for the purposes of general history. Diogenes Laertius may be placed in the same class, but in a very limited degree. Polybius was an author of great talents. His works are principally historical, great part of which have been lost, but in some of the extracts which have been preserved we find essays on government which are very interesting. He lived at the times of Scipio Africanus, and although a Greek, resided at Rome, at a period when the character of the Roman Government was fully unfolded, and by whose example he was enabled to present some features distinct from those which are to be found in Aristotle. His work, however, is strictly characteristic of that epoch. Considering the work of Aristotle as the most comprehensive, systematic, and truly descriptive of the governments of that epoch; of the state of the science, and of the manners of the people, I shall take from it the sketches which I deem material for the object which I have in view.

The work of this author, to which I allude, is called, as has been observed, his Essay on Politics or the Science of Government.

He commences this work in the elementary form, which was adopted by Plato in his two projects, with the origin of society, and in the smallest number of which it can consist. Man and wife form the first stage,[9] father and children the second,[10] master and slave the third.[11] In the first the power is marital; in the second paternal; but in both limited. In the third it is absolute. He asserts that in each it is founded in nature. He then traces the origin of a city with equal minuteness. Into these details I shall not enter, because the opinion with us is too well formed in each instance to require it, and because, likewise, whether his doctrine be well founded or otherwise, no light can be derived from that incipient stage, either as to the organization or the endowment of a government which is necessary to protect liberty and maintain order over the very populous communities of the present day. I think proper to notice only that feature in it which relates to slavery, as it was known to and practiced in the ancient republics. As slavery exists in many of the states of our Union, and involves political considerations of very high importance to those states, and in consequence to the whole Union, I may, in the prosecution of this work, deem it proper to notice it, and it is on that presumption that I make the exception.

It has already been observed that Aristotle made four species of Democracy, four of Aristocracy, four of Oligarchy, and five of Monarchy. It is proper to add that he made a fifth class of government, which he called a Republic, and separated it by certain shades of difference from the others. Of his definition of each species of these several classes of government, I will endeavor to convey a just idea, beginning with Democracy.

---

[9]Diogenes Laertius, Vol. I. Book III. chap. iv.

[10]*Ibid*. Book I. chap. iii.

[11]*Ibid*. chap. iv. p. 188.

The first species of this class, he says, consists of a government in which there is an equality between the rich and the poor, so that neither governs.[12] The second, where the qualification for office in point of revenue is very moderate, and that all who have it are eligible.[13] The third, where every citizen is eligible to office, under the condition that the law, and not the multitude, shall govern.[14] The fourth, is that in which the multitude is the sovereign, and not the law; where the decrees of the multitude at every meeting give the rule, and there is no fixed government or permanent law.[15]

The first species of Aristocracy, he says, is a government which is founded on absolute and not relative virtue, and vested in persons of property. This government, he observes, is the only one in which the virtue of a man of wealth is strictly that of a good citizen. Virtue, in every other instance, he adds, is relative to the kind of government.[16]

His second species is founded on a combination of riches, virtue and liberty.

His third consists of a government which is founded on virtue and liberty without regard to wealth.

The fourth comprehends all the shades of the republic inclining to oligarchy.

His first species of oligarchy is a government which excludes the majority of citizens from office by making the qualification of property so high that few can attain it, but which leaves the door open to all who do.[17] The second, when the revenue required is small, but the appointment to office committed to the magistrates, and in consequence, to those already in office.

The third, when the sons succeed to the offices held by their fathers.

The fourth, when the magistrate is supreme director, without law.[18]

His first species of monarchy consists of a government in which the power of the chief is limited to the perpetual command of the armies, and which may be either elective or hereditary.[19]

The second approaches to tyranny, and is that which is adopted by a certain class of barbarians. It is nevertheless legal, although its forms are

---

[12] Aristotle, Book IV. ch. iv. Vol. I. page 270.
[13] *Ibid.* page 271.
[14] *Ibid.*
[15] *Ibid.*
[16] Aristotle, Book IV. ch. 7, gives his idea of the second species of aristocracy, page 280.
[17] Aristotle, vol. I. Book 4, ch. 5, page 174.
[18] *Ibid.* page 274.
[19] Aristotle, Vol. I. Book III. ch. 10, page 227.

tyrannical, because it is adopted by the consent of the people, is supported by law, and accords with their manners. Of this class he gives the governments and people of Asia as examples. Legitimate monarchy, he says, is that in which submission is voluntary and tyrannical when it is forced. In the one instance the guard, who protects the sovereign, is composed of his subjects, in the others, of foreigners.

His third species is that which was known in the remote ages of Greece, and called Asymnetia. It was tyrannical in its powers, but constituted by the suffrage of the people, and to meet extraordinary emergencies. In some cities it was for life; in others it terminated with the cause which produced it.

The fourth was that of the Jewish ages. It was formed by law and accorded with the manners and will of the people. The chiefs of that age were the benefactors of the people; they led them to victory, instructed them in the arts, and united them in society. Gratitude made them kings, and the consent of the people transmitted the throne to their descendants. They had the supreme direction of every concern relative to war; were chiefs of religion, and judges of the people. By degrees, in the progress of time, some of these relinquished a portion of their power; others were deprived of it by the people.[20]

The fifth species was that of absolute power in an individual, or of despotism.[21]

On a view of these several classes of government, and of the different species of each, the shades of difference between the classes themselves and between the species of each class, and in some instances, between the species of one class and those of another, are so slight, and little regulated by principle, that it is scarcely possible to discriminate between them, or to form a correct idea of his meaning.

Of the first class, that of Democracy, there is less difficulty in comprehending his meaning in each instance than in either of the others. The sovereignty, being admitted to be in the people and the government united with it, and exercised by them en masse, there is no distinction between the several species, as to principle, and little as to the organization. He graduates the several species from that which he considers the best, to the worst, making the condition of the citizens in point of property the basis in each species. The first contemplates such an equality in that respect, that neither the rich nor poor will govern; that such distinct and conflicting classes will not exist; that the whole society will have a common interest.

---

[20]The four species of monarchy are found in Book III. chap. 10.
[21]Book III. chap. 11.

The second forms a slight restraint on the poorer class, by excluding from office those in the most wretched state only, the government being still vested in the whole body of the citizens, and wielded by a majority. The third rejects the distinction by property, and requires simply, that the law shall govern, by which is understood some fixed rule applicable to the whole community, which should be executed with uniformity by the proper tribunals. The fourth places the government exclusively in the hands of the multitude, in which state, he says, that the law is nothing, and their decrees everything. On this last species he descants at large. He represents it as forming a state of anarchy, the most oppressive that can be conceived. The people, he says, are the sovereign, not individually, but in a body; a monarch with a thousand heads.

Of Aristocracy, it is more difficult to comprehend his meaning, either as to the principle on which the government is founded or the different species of which it is composed. His first species consists of a government composed of persons of wealth, and of absolute, not relative, virtue. He does not state how they become possessed of it, whether by hereditary right or election, nor the extent of its powers, nor duration in office, if by election. He supposes these men to be as pure as angels, and to look to no object but the public good, and with consummate wisdom. By relative virtue, it is presumed that he meant governments of the other species and of the other classes, in which those who fill them are ruled by the principles and passions incident to man. It is evident that this species contemplates a government which is altogether theoretical and imaginary, not founded in nature or fact. It cannot therefore be reasoned on, as the principle of any class, or any species of either. Virtue, whether it be of an individual, or of several, can be ascertained by the conduct of the party only. It is not hereditary. A virtuous father often has a vicious son. If dependent on good conduct, there must be some tribunal to judge of it, and the result must depend on the judgment of such tribunal. To reason on a government we must know the principle on which it is founded; how those in office came there, and by what title they hold it, and likewise how it is formed and endowed. As he has not given the necessary information on these points, we cannot view it in any other light than that stated. The same remarks are essentially applicable to his second and third species, the first of which he founds on riches, virtue and liberty; the other on virtue and liberty only. Of wealth as a basis, a distinct idea may be formed, and by liberty, it is understood that he meant the rights of the whole people. If virtue is a visionary basis in one instance, it must be in all others. In founding his fourth species on all the shades of the republic with an inclination of Oligarchy, we must ascertain his meaning by the definition which he gives of those classes, which as to the republic is vague, and as to Oligarchy, explicit in one feature only: that it is a government of the few, and of the rich, in opposition to that of the multitude, and the poor.

The view which he presents of the several species of Oligarchy, confirms the remark which has just been made respecting it. He makes the rich and the few the basis of the class. The qualification for office in the first species is raised so high, that few can attain it. The sum required in the second is diminished, and may be in the third, but as the right is given to those in power in the one to appoint their successors, and as the sons succeeded their fathers in the offices held by them, in the other, the same result might follow. His fourth and last species, consisted of a government in which there was no law other than the will of the magistrate.

From a view of every species of these two classes, of Aristocracy and Oligarchy, it may fairly be inferred, that he did not consider either as hereditary, as holding the government in its own right, and the people as its slaves. If such was the fact, the declaration of it would fix the grade and character of the government, and there could be but one species. In making the shades of difference between the several species of each class he shows that there was nothing settled in either, and that in the contentions for power between ancient families and the body of the people, between the rich and the poor, some of those governments in which the former had gained the ascendancy were better than others. In every instance in which the right of the class depended on the qualification by property, or on any contigency, it may be presumed that the decision rested with the opposite class, the people, and, in consequence, that the government, if not elective, was not strictly hereditary.

The same difficulty occurs in discriminating between his different species of Monarchy. The power in the first was confined to the command of the armies, and might be elective or hereditary. In this species, the chief had no share in the government. His second, although absolute, he deemed legal, being adopted by the consent of the people, and accordant with their manners. He illustrates his idea of this species by the example of the government and people of Asia. By the term legal, it is presumed that he meant that they were made so, by the voluntary submission of the people; that he did not mean to convey the idea, that such governments were free, or any idea respecting the principles of government, or the character of the people themselves. Voluntary submission to such a government is a proof only that the people were competent to none other; that they were fitted only to be slaves. His third species was that which existed in the earliest ages of Greece. It was elective, and in some instances for life; in others for special emergencies with which it terminated. This government, he says, was legal, although tyrannical, because it was the only one to which the people of that age were competent. The same remark is applicable to this species as to the preceding one, with this difference, that it was in all instances elective, and the people in consequence not slaves; the species being attributable to the early and rude age in which it was known. His fourth species applied to the Jewish ages, and had its origin in like manner with those of the third, in the good will and choice of the people. At this period the population of the states had increased, and the manners of the people undergone some change. The call for a more stable and efficient government became, in consequence, proportionally more urgent, while the science had not experienced a corresponding improvement. His fifth species is that of Absolute Monarchy, and which he delineates at great length, reviewing the different species, and explaining the distinctions between them. On the examples which he gives of this class, I shall remark only, that it cannot fail to excite surprise that he should place in it governments that were elective, as those of the first, third and fourth species were, and more especially those in which the term of service of the incumbent might be, for a very short period, a year or less, dependent on the emergency which gave birth to it. The surprise must be equally great to find that he considered the despotism of Asia legal, and for the sole reason, that the people were incompetent to any other.

The view above presented, taken from the work of Aristotle, gives in my estimation, a just representation of the origin of the governments and of the changes which took place in them; of the causes which produced those changes; of the state of society, and likewise of the science of government, during the first epoch. All the governments originated then in monarchy, and were of a limited character, called for by the exigencies of the society, and not claimed by any right in the incumbents. The people were free, and their rulers their instruments, rather than their masters. The descendants of those first advanced to power set up higher claims, which in the progress of time, produced contentions and changes in the government of every state. Of nobility, as a distinct hereditary order, entitled to a share in the sovereignty by hereditary right, no clear and satisfactory evidence is seen. That such a class existed, and often participated in the governments is certain, and that it might be hereditary in some, probable. This class, in every state, seems to have taken its origin in the families of the princes of the early ages who were rich, and whose wealth descended to their posterity, of which the Heraclidae, Pelopidae, etc., furnish examples. When the government by princes was overthrown, the power of the nobility, which was an appendage to it, experienced essentially the same fate. They were however rich, and the mass of the people being poor, and government indispensable, and the people in the states most free having never enjoyed the right to originate any proposition, or any other right than to decide on those which were presented to them from the other branches, and having no talent to institute a free government on sound principles, they remained in the same degraded state which they had held in all preceding ages. The communities were small, and neither extreme, either of liberty or slavery, could be tolerated, or was practicable; for when the power was wrested from the princes by the people they could not exercise it en masse, the only form then known to them, and hence every possible variety was assumed. Aristotle, in the collection which he made of the constitutions of one hundred and fifty-eight people, described what he saw, or of which examples were given, and within which scope he confined his digest. His organization of the different powers of government, with the revolutions to which they were respectively subject, and the means of averting them, extends to every class of free government, and to every species of each class then known. To these causes it is to be attributed that the shades of difference, in point of principle, between the several classes of government are so slight, and in the modification of the several species of each class, in some instances, scarcely perceptible. His work, however, according to the limit within which he moved, does honor to his fame, and will, in many views, and in all ages, be instructive and useful. He gave by full illustration, the example only of the Governments of Lacedemon, Crete, Carthage, and Athens, which he thought the best of their kind.

I will now proceed to take a like view of the works of the writers of the second epoch, among which those of Locke, Sydney, Montesquieu and Rousseau are particularly entitled to attention. A long space had intervened between the writers of those two epochs, which was, especially after the overthrow of the Roman Empire, an interval of barbarism and darkness. In both epochs the contest was for liberty on the part of the people. In the first, it was between the two extremes, the multitude and individuals. What were the rights of kings, what of the nobility, what of the people, were the great questions in both, and the distinction between the classes, especially the two latter, did not apply so much in the first to hereditary right in the nobility, as between the rich and the poor. The governments which were founded on the ruins of the Roman Empire were in their origin comparatively free, but they soon terminated, especially with the principal powers, in despotism. From that state Europe began to emerge when those authors appeared. The old system, with all its changes, was before them, and to it the new had added nothing, by any example it afforded, to the improvement of the science itself. The modern governments were more simple. The territory of each community was of vast extent, as was its population, compared with those of Greece, and the classes in society were more completely separated from each other. The approach to despotism was rapid, and its continuance of long duration, because in countries of such extent the power of the people was soon lost, and in their unlettered and ignorant state they had no means of recovering it. The power of the nobility was too feeble to form any check on the career of the prince. The rights of that corps, however, were more distinct than in any of the ancient governments. Wherever it existed, whether it held the government exclusively in its hands, or belonged to absolute monarchy, it was hereditary. In the latter governments it was a mere appendage to the prince, having no rights in opposition to his, but it supported his power in contests with the people, because in so doing, it supported its own, holding immense possessions, and the people, in a state of vassalage, under them. The people of England were the first who put seriously to issue the great principles on which free government turned; and these authors may be considered, and especially those of that country, the first who took the lead in their illustration and support.

The works of the two first mentioned writers were composed at a period very interesting to this country, as it likewise was to that of their own. It was one of great commotion, produced by a contest for power between the friends of liberty on the one side, and of despotism on the other. The English nation had then reached a stage when in the progress of society, some fixed and permanent form to its government had become indispensable, and which must terminate in a complete revolution in favor of the one or other party, or in a compromise between them. To produce either result, great contention violence and civil war were inevitable. These conflicts were connected with the emigration and settlement of our ancestors in these states, and with the great events which have since followed in them. The works of these writers, therefore, are interesting to us in two views. They are so in reference to the nature of the governments which then existed throughout Europe, and of the state of society, and of the science at the time. They are so likewise, from the influence which that state and the convulsions which followed in their own country had on the emigration of a portion of its inhabitants to this territory, and on the career and fortune of their descendants. The general characteristics of this epoch have been described. All the ancient republics had been overthrown, and a new state of affairs introduced and established throughout Europe. Different forms of government were established, and the whole system changed.

Locke's work occupies about 150 pages, folio, and is divided into two books, the first of which contains an examination and refutation of a work of Sir Robert Filmer, which was written in favor of the divine right of kings. The second forms a regular essay on civil government. In the first, he states the doctrine of Filmer, in full extent, with his argument in support of it, and refutes it by scriptural authority and sound reasoning. In the second he traces the origin of government to its true source the consent of the people and the equal rights of all. He speaks of the different classes of government, Democracy, Monarchy and Oligarchy, omitting that of Aristocracy, but which, it is presumed, he comprised in Oligarchy. He treats also of mixed governments.

Mr. Locke contemplates, as other writers do, two distinct ages in society; the one, the early and rude age; the other, the more advanced and civilized state. In the first, he admits that government originates, generally, in an individual, and may be paternal, but contends, that in every period of that age it is elective and free. In both ages, he considers the people as the source of power, and having an inalienable right to give to the government what form they please. If they tolerate a bad one, it is either because they are incompetent to any other, or are prevented from making a change by other causes.[22] In all that he advances in favor of the rights of the people, his view is unquestionably correct, and is supported with great ability; but it is confined to the epoch specified, and to the governments which characterized it. The Feudal system, which had been founded by the nations who had overthrown the Roman Empire, and established themselves on its ruins, precluded, especially among the principal powers, all idea of self-government.

In treating of the organization of a government, and the manner in which the people must exercise their power, in case of abuse, we see distinctly that he had the British Constitution in view. He considers the legislature as the supreme power of the state, comprising the House of Commons, the House of Peers, and the king. That it comprehends the three branches is inferred from the fact, that each has a participation in its powers; the king by a negative on the laws, and likewise by a distinction which he makes between an executive magistrate who has that power, and one who has not. The former he places on elevated ground above the laws; the latter he considers subject to be changed and displaced at pleasure.[23] In this he concurs with Blackstone, who says that the Parliament is omnipotent. It is only in governments which recognize distinct orders, of the class called free, that the legislative power can be viewed in that light. In those of that class, the government is united with the sovereignty, and in consequence

---

[22]Book II. chap. 8, section 105.
[23]*Ibid.* chap. 13, sections 151-2; again, chap. 17, section 23.

there can be no check on them within the limit of the constitution. There can be none, except by popular movements and the overthrow of the government itself. In supporting the power of the legislature, he supports that of the people against that of the kings, because it is in the legislature that the people exercise their power in the government; and in asserting that the people have the right to rise en masse and overthrow the government, in the case of abuse, he supports the doctrine, that all power originates in the people, whatever be the form of the government, or great the power of the kings.

In his definitions of the powers of government, we see no nice discrimination of those which should be vested in the executive and judiciary. In treating of prerogative, we find that he allows to the executive the power to regulate the number of members in every county or borough entitled to representation, as the population may increase or diminish; and likewise to establish new corporations, and fix the number of representatives to each.[24] In this he transcends our idea of the power which should be held by that branch, even under our free representative government. We think that it should be vested in the legislature only. The objection to the exercise of it by an hereditary prince is much stronger, since by the abuse of the power, which should always be guarded against, he might multiply the dependents on him and thereby increase his influence. He says nothing in favor of the independence of the judiciary. On the contrary, by giving to it no power over an unconstitutional law, the legislature being supreme, he makes it subservient to that branch, and in consequence, to the ruling power in the state.

Mr. Locke's work was written with great ability, and was certainly very interesting and useful to his country, and as may be presumed, to Europe, at the time it was written. He touches no subject which he does not thoroughly analyze, nor advance any doctrine which he does not fully illustrate and ably support. But whoever examines it with attention, will find that there is little in it other than the support which he gives to the general cause of liberty, which can be considered applicable to us. His refutation of the work of Filmer, in favor of the divine right of kings, may certainly be viewed in this light. No one here has a claim to that station, or ever had, nor does any one entertain that sentiment. This remark is equally applicable to his argument in favor of the right of the people to change their government at pleasure, and to punish those who violate the laws, or are otherwise guilty of misconduct. There is no difference of sentiment on these points with us. All our governments are founded on

---

[24]Book II. chap. 13, section 158.

that principle, and have been in practical and successful operation since the Declaration of our Independence. Mr. Locke's work may, therefore, be viewed in the light in which I have placed it; as characteristic of the epoch at which it was written; as exhibiting a true picture of the nature of the governments, the state of society, and of the science at the time. He does not look at the dangers to which our system is exposed, nor suggest the means of averting them. It is proper to add, that if it was difficult, and almost impossible to sustain the mixed form of which the British Government was composed, the preservation of one founded on the sovereignty of the people could not have been even thought of by those most friendly to liberty. This remark is justified by Mr. Locke himself, for it is manifest from the whole work, that such was his opinion, and may fairly be inferred, that he thought a mixed government, such as that of Great Britain, resting on its true principles, the best that could be established.

The principles which were cherished by this very able writer and virtuous man, rendered him obnoxious to the Court, and of which he felt the ill effect. He was a fellow of Christ Church College in the University of Oxford, and from which he was expelled, by the special order of the king, Charles the Second.

The view which has been taken of the work of Locke is equally applicable to that of Sydney, in reference to the objects of this inquiry. It was written to refute the doctrine of Filmer, in favor of the divine right of kings, and of which he never loss sight in any part of his essay, which comprises two volumes, octavo, of about 400 pages each. It furnishes a complete refutation of that doctrine, and likewise demonstrates, that the power of princes, however great or long its continuance, is derived from the consent of the people, and sustained afterwards when it assumes an oppressive character, by their inability to remove it. It is, however, not confined to these objects. He enters with great ability into a comparison of the merits of governments in which the people hold a portion of the sovereignty, and are free, with those which are absolute, and in which they are slaves. In the one, he gives examples of every great and noble quality that can adorn the human race and exalt the character of the community; in the other, of those only which show the degradation and decrepitude of man; of nothing but what is calculated to excite our mortification and disgust. His work displays a profound knowledge of ancient and modern history, and may be considered, in the view stated, as one of the most able ever written in favor of free government against despotism. There is scarcely an individual, of those most distinguished in any of the ancient republics, or of modern times, down to his own period, to whose talents and virtues he does not pay the respect to which they are entitled. But beyond this limit I do not perceive that his work extends. In several passages, he avows explicitly his preference of a government composed of three (3) orders, a king, lords and commons, to one founded exclusively on the sovereignty of people.[25] In this, however, it may be inferred that he had in view those only of the latter class, in which the people exercised their power en masse. None, like our own, ever existed before; and of course he could contemplate none of which history had furnished no example.

Sydney looked to the dangers which menaced liberty in his own country, and as Locke did to the means of preserving it, on the principles of the British Constitution, to which he thought the people competent, if roused to make the necessary exertion. Tyranny had existed; civil war had ensued; a king had been overthrown and beheaded; a commonwealth had been established; but under circumstances which proved that liberty was not secure even under it; the family of Stuart had been restored, and with increased danger to the great cause to which he was devoted. It could not be expected, under these circumstances, that Sydney would look beyond his own country, or to other objects, than such as were connected with the existing crisis. In defense of those, he exerted his best efforts and displayed great talents, and to that great cause he fell a victim.

When it is considered that such men as Locke and Sydney found it necessary and were compelled to devote their talents and labors to the refutation of so absurd a doctrine as that of the divine right of kings, most of whom then reigning, or of their families, had been placed by casual events at the head of their respective governments, what an impression must it make on all reflecting minds, of the state of society at the epoch at which they lived? If such were the prejudices, superstition and darkness of the age, to make it difficult to convince the people that they had any rights, and were not born slaves, how idle must it have been to have drawn their attention to the organization and distribution of power, in self-government, with its various modifications, and to the dangers to which a failure, in any of those respects, would expose it.

The works of Montesquieu and Rousseau merit a like commendation with that which has been bestowed on those of Locke and Sydney. They were written in another country, under a government in a different state, and, in consequence, in a different spirit. The work of Montesquieu is called the Spirit of Laws, and it corresponds with the title; but as the laws must depend on, and be adapted to the nature and principle of the government under which they are formed, it became necessary to give a distinct idea of each class in all its most important features. This he has executed

---

[25]Vol. I. chap. i. section 10: chap. ii. section 16.

with great ability, and in support of which, he brings into view all the ancient governments, and likewise the modern down to his own time. There is no subject which falls within the scope of legislation, under any species of government, and in every part of the globe, which escapes his attention, and on which he does not make very interesting remarks. His work, therefore, may be considered, as embracing, according to his view, the circle of the science, with the examples in support of it, which history had then afforded. In the range which he has taken, it is obvious that there are many subjects on which he treats, to which no attention is necessary on my part. Whatever he says of despotic governments, and of the laws that are adapted to them, is of this character. The same remark is applicable to mixed governments, and indeed to every class; for if self-government is sound in principle, and merits the opinion entertained of it, under the improvement it has received with us, those who execute it will adopt the laws correspondent therewith, and necessary to its support. My object relates to that point, and in referring to the works of different writers, I do it to show that they apply to governments differently circumstanced, and that so far as liberty is an object, and cherished by them, there is not only nothing discouraging in their works to our system, but everything in its support.

Montesquieu occupied different ground from that which had been held by Locke or Sydney. He was not a party to any existing conflict, and saw the improvement which had been given to the British Government by that, for their services in promoting which both had suffered, and one fallen a victim. He had with them all the advantages which could be derived from the examples of the ancient republics, and the science of the ancient world, and likewise of the modern, aided by the improvement in the government referred to, and by their works in support of that great cause. His work is very favorable to liberty, and has given much support to it, but living under a despotic government caution was necessary on his part. It was, therefore, of a nature so elementary, extended to so many objects unconnected with it, and was written in a spirit of such moderation, that it could not be considered an attack on his own government.

In his view of the ancient republics, and of governments generally, he rejects the classification which had been given of them by Aristotle, as he likewise does the number of species which he ascribes to each class. He notices his first species of Monarchy, which he considers visionary, being founded on the good or ill-conduct of the incumbent, and not on principle.[26] His view is more simple than that of the ancient authors, arising from the

---

[26]Book XI. chap. ix.

character of the Feudal system; but it does not extend to the precise objects of this inquiry, and in some points which involve general principles, is not free from objection. This, however, may fairly be attributed to the state of the science at the time, and to the nature and form of the government to which, in comparison with all others, he gave the preference.

In treating of Democracy he contemplated that only which was known to the ancients, in which the people exercised their power, en masse, and the government was united with the sovereignty. Whatever he says of this class of government, is under this impression, and can, in consequence, refer only to the defects of that state, and not to the improvements of the present day by representation.[27] Such a government would be impracticable, as will be shown, even for a small state. For a large one it could not have been thought of.

In the view which he took of the Constitution of England, and his remarks on it, it is obvious that he considered it the most that perfect human wisdom could devise. That it was the best then known I readily admit; but that it is inferior to our own, is, according to my judgment, certain. As I propose to treat of this government, and to make a comparison between it and those of the United States hereafter, it is unnecessary, and it would be improper to enter into the subject here.

He observes that the constitution may be free, and the citizen not: that the citizen may be free, and the constitution not.[28] From this it may be inferred, that he meant that liberty does not depend altogether on the government, and his illustration of the idea does not preclude the inference. It must now be obvious, that the liberty of the citizen depends solely on the government, and that if the government be founded on just principles, and be in the hands of a virtuous and intelligent people, he cannot fail to enjoy liberty. Such a people will always see that such laws are made, and are so executed, as in a manner to secure to every citizen the enjoyment of that blessing. It is also equally obvious, that if the government be absolute, the people must be slaves. A virtuous and humane prince might not molest them, but as their security and peace would depend on his will they could have no rights of their own. Objections occur to other passages in this work, but it does not fail within the limit of this inquiry to enter into the subject in that view. Many of these have been shown by Mr. De Tracy, a French writer of talents, in a work which will, I doubt not, be read with great attention and satisfaction by those who peruse that on which

---

[27]Book II. chap. i.
[28]Book XII. chap. i.

it is a commentary. On a view of the whole work it certainly merits the commendation which has been bestowed on it.

The work of Rousseau, to which attention is next due, is entitled the Social Compact. It traces government to the people, and maintains with great force that none is legitimate, which is not founded on their consent. The manner in which the compact is formed, when regularly entered into, its extent and the obligation which it imposes on the people who are parties to it, are treated with ability, and the work, taken in all its parts, is consistent with itself, and an able essay. It is obvious that he was thoroughly acquainted with ancient and modern history, and with the works of the writers of both epochs on the subject of government.

He explicitly avows his opinion that the government should be vested in and be exercised by the people collectively, in a general assembly, and in consequence be united with the sovereignty. He maintains the doctrine that the sovereignty cannot be represented.[29] Every law which the people do not pass themselves he considers void. The people of England, he says, think that they are free, but they deceive themselves. They are free only while engaged in the election of members to Parliament, and as soon as that act is performed, they are slaves.[30] He asserts that the idea of representation is modern, and derived from the Feudal system, by which the human race are degraded, and the name of man dishonored. He adds that in the ancient republics the people had no representatives: that even the term was unknown to them.[31]

His whole work is founded on this principle, and the organization which he gives to the government, and the distribution of its powers, correspond with it. The legislative power is vested in a general assembly of the people, without the aid of any other branch, to digest measures for their consideration or to form a check on their decision. He contemplates an executive distinct from the legislature, but as forming in effect no part of the government, its members being merely commissaries or agents under it. Respecting the judiciary, he makes no comment, nor does he propose any plan for the performance of that portion of the public duties, in questions arising either between the citizens themselves or between the government and the citizens. The legislature, according to his view, held the sovereignty of the state. When the people were assembled, the government in all its functions was suspended.[32] The magistrates became members of that body

---

[29]Book III. chap. xv. Vol. II. page 185.
[30]*Ibid.* page 186.
[31]*Ibid.*
[32]Book III. chap. xiv. Vol. II. page 161.

with no other rights or authority than belonged to every other citizen. Every power was concentrated in a general assembly of the people. He made some nice distinctions between those powers which that assembly would exercise, calling one portion, such as were of a general nature, and applied to the whole community, acts of sovereignty; and such as related to special objects, or to individuals, the acts of magistrates, giving thus to the same body, and to the same man, in the discharge of their ordinary duties, a different character.[33] He was aware that such a government could apply only to a state of very limited extent and population; to a village, and little more; and that it would be exposed to imminent danger, both internal and external. For these evils he suggests a remedy, by extraneous and temporary provisions, such as the Tribunate of Rome, or the Ephori of Sparta, and in great emergencies of a dictatorship. The plan of this writer was evidently founded on that of the ancient republics, with some modifications which experience, aided by his reflections, had suggested. It is obvious that he considered the alternative to be between the government of the people en masse and that in which they were to hold a very limited portion of power only, to form what was called the tiers etats or third estate; and that he preferred the former. Having been born in Geneva, a small state, it may be inferred that he took his impressions in part from that circumstance; and in many respects his plan accords with that of Athens, one of those with which I propose to compare our system. As therefore all the remarks which I shall make on that government will apply to this sketch, it will be unnecessary to make further comments on it.

I might, with propriety, notice the works of other writers, and particularly of Machiavel and De Lolme; the first of whom composed an essay on the first decade of Livy, and the other on the Constitution of England, both of which display talent. But as they relate to the two preceding epochs, and not to the third, it is deemed unnecessary to enter on them. When I reach the subjects on which they treat I may advert to them. The works of the writers to which I have referred are sufficient for my object. They give a clear and distinct idea of the state of society, of the governments, and of the science in the first two epochs, which was my motive for referring to them. They confirm the opinion advanced, that the contest on the part of the people in the first was for the whole power to be exercised by them en masse; and in the second, that it was to prevent their entire exclusion from the government in any and every form whatever; to rescue themselves from abject slavery.

In reference to the second epoch, and to Great Britain, whose people

---

[33]Chap. xvii.

took the lead among the great powers in support of human rights, I think proper to insert here a comment from the posthumous works of an enlightened patriot and great statesman, Mr. Fox, which confirms the view taken of the character of that epoch, and of the dangers incident to it. The struggle to which I allude was that during which the works of Locke and Sydney were composed, and which commenced in the reign of Charles the First, of the family of Stuart, and in which all hope of success depended on the part which the House of Commons might act in it. In adverting to that crisis, he states the following propositions, which all people should constantly have in view who may be engaged in such a struggle, or who may be blessed with free governments of the best kind. Under the excitement of party feeling, those who take the lead on each side have it much in their power to abuse the confidence of the people, especially if the controversy be carried to great extent, and of which they seldom fail to take advantage, and for the worst purposes. He asks, "In what manner will that house conduct itself? will it be content with its regular share of legislative power, and with the influence which it cannot fail to possess, whenever it exerts itself upon the other branches of the legislative and executive power? or will it boldly (perhaps rashly) pretend to a power commensurate with the natural rights of the representatives of the people? If it should, will it not be obliged to support its claims by military force? And how long will such a force be under its control? How long before it follows the usual course of all armies, and ranges itself under a single master? If such a master should arise, will he establish an hereditary or an elective government? If the first, what will be gained by a change of dynasty? If the second, will not the military power, as it chose the first king or protector (the name is of no importance), choose in effect all his successors? Or will he fail, and shall we have a restoration, usually the most dangerous and worst of all revolutions?" These interrogatories contemplate the great epochs of such a struggle, with the means by which the people, in case they succeed and overthrow their antagonist, may be made in each and every stage, by the abuse of their confidence, by those who take the lead on their side, the instruments of their own destruction. They afford a very strong proof of the enlightened mind of a practical statesman who watched with care the dangers to which the great cause to which he was devoted was exposed. They apply particularly to the state in which the people of England then were; but the example to which they refer must be instructive to all people, under every species of free government. The work of this writer was not finished, which is much to be regretted, since had it been completed it cannot be doubted that it would have shed much light on every branch of the subject to which it might have extended.

The people of England held their station in the House of Commons, and they were the only people of any great power in Europe who enjoyed that advantage at that period. That hold enabled them to prostrate every order in the state, because they moved with vast force and with great energy to the accomplishment of that result. In suffering their leader to take essentially the station of the chief whom they had deposed and beheaded, they furnish a strong proof that they were incompetent to the support of a government which belonged exclusively to themselves. If any doubt existed on that point, the restoration to the throne of a member of the same family soon after the decease of that leader would remove it. It is proper to add that Mr. Fox, in speaking in terms of high commendation of the works of Locke and Sydney, gives a further confirmation of the difference between that and the preceding epoch, by observing that they had never conceived the wild project of assimilating the Government of England to that of Athens, of Sparta, or of Rome.

The third epoch is that, as has been observed, which is marked by the emigration of our ancestors to this territory, by the Revolution which followed, and the governments which have been erected on its basis, in all of which the sovereignty is vested in the people, but the government separated from it and committed to representative bodies. This epoch is, therefore, altogether different from the others. The governments being different, the dangers which menace them are likewise so. Happily they are in all respects of inferior magnitude. Such dangers however do, and will exist, which ought to be understood and guarded against. The principles and passions of men are always the same, and lead to the same result, varying only according to the circumstances in which they are placed. Self-interest is the ruling passion, whether under free or despotic governments. Highly improved and generous minds will move on a scale correspondent therewith, but a large portion of mankind will look to themselves, and turn every incident of which they may take advantage to their own account. It is against these propensities that we have to guard. The principle of the government will go far to infuse a correct spirit into the body of the people, and will have great influence on those who are appointed to high and honorable trusts, provided the people perform, with judgment, their essential duties. A failure, and even a relaxation on their part, may produce the worst consequences. If they make judicious selections for office, reward those who have merit, and punish those who commit offenses: if they act for themselves, are intelligent, impartial and firm, and do not become the instruments of others, the whole movement cannot fail to be mild, harmonious and successful.

In what relates to the ancient world, we read with peculiar interest the history of the ancient republics, and particularly of those specified. Indeed there is nothing beyond that limit, relating to that epoch, in which we take a serious interest. The career of despotic governments viewed internally exhibits a gloomy spectacle; and externally, even where talents are displayed, by their respective chiefs, being generally of a military character, and employed in the subjugation and oppression of other people, although it may excite a species of admiration, it cannot give pleasure. The people are held by such governments in a state of degradation and oppression, deprived of opportunities of displaying those noble and generous qualities which do honor to the human race. Their conduct is watched in every circumstance, and reported by a vigilant and active police. High qualities are dreaded. But in republics, even in those in which the people enjoy a portion of the sovereignty only, a different state of things exists, and a different spectacle is exhibited. The society moves itself. The springs of action are within it. Great virtues and talents, wherever found, exalt the possessors, and increase the energy and stability of the government. Notwithstanding all the disadvantages to which the ancient republics were subject, we find in them a greater display of all the higher qualities of talent and virtue, more to gratify our feelings, to command our admiration and applause, than in the history of every other people from the earliest record of time. Their rise and progress form a great epoch in the history of the world. Under their protection the arts and sciences flourished, and the human mind acquired an expansion never known before. With their overthrow universal darkness overspread the earth, and held it in ignorance and barbarism for ages. From that degraded state we may date the commencement of its emancipation in several of the countries of Europe, with that of the sixteenth century, which was further marked with the discovery of this hemisphere. That great event paved the way to our Revolution, which laid the foundation of a system of government under circumstances more favorable to success than were ever enjoyed by any of the ancient republics, and with the light derived from their example, with the best means of correcting their errors and avoiding their fate.

The discovery of this hemisphere was made in a spirit of philosophic calculation and speculation, and on the part of those who first embarked in it of adventure; but the emigrants who soon followed, and who laid the foundation of the communities which have since grown up in these states, were persons of enlarged views and elevated character. Although of different political parties and of different religious sects in the parent country, yet they all flew from persecution, in pursuit of liberty, and they inculcated that sentiment on their descendants. In the convulsions to which the British Government was then subject, and the transition of power from one order to another, the cause of emigration, in the masses who came over, was different, but the moral effect soon became uniform. It is known that two of the regicides, if not more, were buried in the Eastern States, and that Cromwell himself was at one time prepared to fly. And incidents occur, even at this late day, to show that many of distinction of the opposite party found then an asylum in the Middle and Southern States. The immediate emigrants, therefore, felt this difference sensibly, but in the new relation which was formed between them and between the colonies and the parent country, that feeling subsided, and was unknown to their descendants. The charters under which they emigrated, which formed a compact between the people and the crown, nursed the infant state and reared it to maturity under the influence of free principles. Distinct orders were precluded. All the emigrants and their descendants were placed on a footing of equality. Had those of the highest rank in England visited any of the colonies without commissions authorized by their charters they would have held the grade only of private individuals. Had the king himself come over, he could have taken the place only in the colony in which he landed, of his governor. Thus successive generations grew up in each colony in the same principles, and bearing the same common relation to the crown, the only extraneous power which was recognized. As its pressure was felt, and other pretensions were advanced, the whole people were gradually drawn together by the powerful bond of interest and affections, so that when the revolutionary struggle commenced, they moved in a body as a single community.

The elevation of mind which was brought over by those emigrants was never lost; but by the operation of the causes stated was infused into the mass of each community. There never was a period when an appeal was made to the talents and virtue of the inhabitants of the colonies, notwithstanding the difficulties they had to encounter, in making their establishments in the new world, that indicated the least inferiority between them and those of the old. Their conduct in the war of 1756 extorted that confession in their favor from the government of the parent country, and the display which was made in both respects in the war of the Revolution commanded the applause, not only of the first men there, but of the whole civilized world. In these very important circumstances, therefore, the good people of these states enjoyed advantages, which there is good reason to believe were peculiar to themselves; advantages which could not fail to have the happiest effect in enabling to form, as well as to sustain, the governments which have been instituted.

In forming our governments the question of city and country, of the rich and the poor, could never have come into view. By the charters to the colonies vast territories were granted, and a great proportion thereof in each was settled before the commencement of the contest. As the population had increased and moved westward, each colony was laid off into counties, from which representatives were sent, to a general assembly in each. The power of the colony was in the hands of this assembly, and in consequence, of the country, the cities having their equal share in it, which was scarcely felt as such in any colony. The poor as a class, organized against the rich, was unknown, and still is. The aged and infirm, who are indigent, are provided for in every county, in every state, with houses, food, clothes, and medical aid, at the expense of the other citizens of the county. The claim is founded on motives of charity, which there is no necessity either to withhold or to carry beyond its just limits. The great mass of our population, consisting of persons who were neither very poor nor very rich, a discrimination, in any form, to protect the one against the other could not have been thought of. The sovereignty being in the people, the door might be left open with perfect safety, to every citizen, to every office, and without distinction as to the right of suffrage, other than such as marked him as an inhabitant of the county or township, with such small interest there as should enable him to act as a free agent.

The good people of these states have, therefore, been placed in a situation to make a fair experiment of the great problem, whether the people, as a people, are competent to self-government. All the circumstances with which they are blessed, more favorable to such a result than were ever enjoyed by any other people, impose on them, in like degree, the greater obligation to succeed. Satisfied I am that success is not only practicable, but certain, if equal virtue and talents are displayed in future with those which have brought us to the present age.

To do justice to the subject, it will be proper in regard to our system to extend the inquiry in like manner to its origin, and to the great events which have so far marked its career. From such a view, a fair comparison may be made of our governments, state and national, with those referred to, and a correct estimate be formed of the merits and defects of our own in both its branches. A like comparison may be made of the state of society on each side, and a fair conclusion be drawn of the competency of our people to self-government. We have had divisions which have disturbed the harmony, and at certain epochs, excited great inquietude as to the future. To what causes were these imputable? An impartial and candid statement of facts can injure no one individually, and may be useful to our country. Passions have long since subsided, and such is the state of the public mind, and even of those who felt and acted under the greatest excitement, that they can now look back with moderation and calmness on the past, and profit by the instruction it affords. Having been an active party in many of the most interesting scenes, I am aware that I may have taken impressions in some instances that were unfounded. Should this be the case, the view which I may present will be open to correction: and if, in any instance, I be in error, I wish to be corrected. My great object is the success of our system in both its branches, because I well know that on it the happiness of the whole nation depends. In pursuit of this object I have no feeling of resentment to any one to gratify; and am far from wishing to detract from the fame, or wound the feelings of those with whom I differed, many of whom had, in council and in the field, deserved well of their country.

ATHENS

It is impossible to proceed in the comparison of our governments with those of Greece, either State or National, without being forcibly struck with the difference between them in all those circumstances which are most important. There is not one, either in the extent of territory, the number of inhabitants, the state of society, the manner of instituting the government, its organization, or the distribution of its powers, in which there is the least similitude. Athens, comprising Attica, contained a territory not larger than several of the counties in some of our states. Lacedemon was not more extensive than the smallest state in our Union, and all Greece was smaller than Scotland or Portugal. The difference in the other circumstances enumerated was equally great, and still more important. These differences must be taken into view and have their due weight in the prosecution of this work.

The Government of Athens, of which I propose to treat, is that which was instituted by Solon nearly five hundred years before the Christian era. In that government many ancient regulations were incorporated, some of which had been adopted about one thousand years before, and had formed a part of the existing government in all its subsequent changes. In adopting those regulations, Solon must have done it, either because he believed them to be correct, or was satisfied that the community was so wedded to them by habit and prejudice, that it would tolerate no government of which they should not form a part. When the nature of those institutions is considered, it might fairly be inferred that the latter was the cause. The fact, however, was established by himself, he having declared that he had formed for the people of Athens, not the government which he deemed the best, but the best which he thought they were capable of sustaining. By this it appears, that in the formation of the government he considered the condition of the people, their state of civilization, their weaknesses and vices, with their intelligence and virtues. To judge correctly of the considerations which induced their adoption in the first instance, and their preservation afterwards, we must go back to the epoch at which they were adopted, and view the condition of the people at that period and in every subsequent stage. A slight knowledge of mankind will show that the con-

74

dition of the people at any advanced period could not have been formed at the moment, but must have been the result of many causes operating on the community from its commencement.

Historians carry the origin of this people back to a very remote period. They nevertheless all agree in fixing on one beyond which nothing occurred that merits attention. In regard to Athens the reign of Cecrops forms that period, which, according to the most authentic chronology, occurred more than sixteen hundred years before the birth of Christ and about two thousand three hundred and fifty after the creation of the world. Cecrops emigrated from Egypt and settled in Attica, taking with him many of his countrymen, whom he incorporated into the same community with the natives, placing himself, by common consent, at their head. Before that period it is stated by the best informed historians that the inhabitants of Attica were barbarians; that they dwelt in caves, and fed on the rude productions of the earth and on game. The inhabitants of Egypt were more advanced in civilization, and in the arts and usages of civilized life, than those of Greece. Such improvements as existed in Egypt Cecrops transplanted with him into his newly adopted country. The motive for union between the parties was strong. The one sought an asylum, the other instruction.

All that region known by the name of ancient Greece was at that epoch in the same state, and the greater part of it, not the whole, owed the commencement of its improvement to the same cause, the arrival and establishment among them of colonies from Egypt, Phoenicia, and the East. Four other colonies are particularly mentioned by historians, one of which was led by Inachus, likewise from Egypt, who settled in Argos; another by Pelops, from Asia, who settled in the Peloponnesus; a third from Phoenicia, by Cadmus, who settled in Boetia; a fourth by Danaus, likewise from Egypt, who settled in Argos. The first preceded Cecrops about three hundred years. The other three followed shortly after him. The leaders of those colonies had each the same fortune which had attended Cecrops, of being placed at the head of the community in which they respectively settled, and for the same reason the superior intelligence which they possessed, and the desire of the people to avail themselves of it.

Thucydides, the author of the "Peloponnesian War," which occurred rather more than one hundred and fifty years after the institution of the Government of Solon, considers the history of Greece as involving no event of real importance, either of a military or political nature, prior to that war. His opinion is the more interesting, because the war with Persia and the invasions by Darius and Xerxes had preceded the Peloponnesian war, the latter a few years only, and had in fact led to it. It justifies the inference which has been drawn from a passage in his work, that he thought that Herodotus had greatly exaggerated the force which had been brought against Greece in those invasions; as it does the opinion entertained of the feeble and effeminate character of the troops and people of Persia, compared with those of Europe. Thucydides states that the war with Troy was the first enterprise in which the Greeks united, and that they were drawn into that war more by the power and influence of Agamemnon, King of Argos, and leader of the expedition, than by any general feeling or policy of their own. That war united them in the expedition, but their union terminated with it, and the absence of the chiefs from their respective dominions had so far impaired their power at home that the efforts they were compelled to make to regain it on their return exhibited scenes of internal commotion and civil war for a long time afterward, in many of the states, of the most frightful character. There was then no regular bond of union between the states, nor were the people known, until a remote subsequent period, by the common name of Greeks. Homer, who composed his poems long after the Trojan war, called those of each state by the name appropriate thereto, Danians, Argives, Acheens, etc. There can be no doubt that that expedition owes its renown more to the splendid genius of Homer, and the poetic license of which he availed himself, than to the talents which were displayed, or to the exploits that were performed in it. The people were uncivilized before the war, and they remained equally so a long time after its conclusion.

The enlightened and faithful historian referred to, confirms the elementary view heretofore presented, founded on the principles, the passions, and the qualities of man, of the origin of societies and of governments over them, in the rude state, and of the incidents to such societies and governments in their progress from that state to a state of civilization. He describes them as unlettered and uncivilized; the states, he says, were small, and their governments for a long time monarchical and hereditary, but with limited authority. The first step to improvement was the Trojan war, and simply by embarking them on the sea, and making them better acquainted with navigation. Piracy ensued, and was long deemed an honorable occupation in all the maritime states, and in some even down to his own time. Tyrannies then grew up, and civil wars were the consequence. His sketch is concise, but it may fairly be concluded from the facts which he states, that the limitation affirmed by him to have existed to the power of the prince in the early stages, proceeded from the manner in which the office originated, and the inability of the people in their rude state to form any other kind of government, or to limit its powers in any precise form or on any just principles. It may also be inferred with equal certainty that the changes which afterwards occurred in those governments, with the contentions and civil wars which attended them, proceeded from the change which had taken place in the pursuits, the names and condition of the people, and which required a more extended legislation and greater vigor in the administration, at a period when the science of government had not experienced a degree of improvement adequate to the object.

A general view of the state of Greece at this early epoch is all that is deemed necessary. I will give a more detailed one of that of Athens, whose government is now the particular object of attention.

The regulations which were adopted by Cecrops corresponded with the barbarous state in which the people of Athens then were, and with the knowledge which he had acquired in Egypt, the country of his nativity. This coast was infested by pirates, and the frontiers by banditti from the neighboring state of Boetia. To protect the people from these invasions, he drew them together into cities, of which twelve were founded; Athens being the principal one. He transplanted the fruits of Egypt into Attica, and trained the inhabitants to agriculture, by showing them the manner, as well as the blessings resulting from it. I give these details, in which all historians agree, merely to show the rude state in which the people then were.

His political institutions, as might naturally be expected, were few. He divided the people into tribes, of which he formed four, and regulated marriages by law. In each of the villages he instituted a species of corporation, with power to administer justice for the inhabitants thereof, and he likewise gave it a council for civil purposes. The power of these bodies approached nearly to a state of independence, and formed in a great measure so many separate republics. Some writers ascribe to him the institution of the Court or Senate of the Areopagus, while others trace it to his son. It certainly owed its origin to that epoch, and whether to the father or the son, in reference to the object in view, is altogether immaterial. This tribunal was charged with criminal offenses, and was preserved through every change which afterwards occurred in the government of Athens, until the time of Solon, who adopted it in his constitution with increased powers.

From the reign of Cecrops to the Constitution of Solon about one thousand years intervened. The reigns of Theseus and Codrus form the most interesting epochs in the history of that people and of their government through that long interval. From Cecrops to Theseus nearly three centuries elapsed, and from the latter to Codrus rather a longer term. The government from the first to the last of these princes continued to be hereditary, during which seventeen had reigned. When Theseus mounted the throne, the power of the prince was unsettled, passing occasionally from one extreme to the other. The progress in science and civilization had been inconsiderable, while in other respects the condition and morals of the people had grown worse. Agriculture, commerce and the arts had been introduced among them, the effect of which was sensibly felt in many ways by every class of society. A portion of the people had become very rich, and another portion very poor. A distinction of ranks had grown up among them, founded on the ascendancy and control which the rich had acquired over the poor, and which was promoted by the nature of the government itself. The spirit of equality and independence which characterized the rude age was broken. With the poor, when not extinguished or smothered by the degradation to which they were subjected, it was seen only in convulsions and insurrections. And with the rich, pretensions of a different character, equally inconsistent with the principles of rational liberty were set up and acted on. The authority of the twelve villages which had been founded by Cecrops had augmented to a great height. They often quarreled with and sometimes made war on each other. The power of the prince alone could control them, and that was often opposed and shaken. Under these circumstances, the tendency was at one time to anarchy, and at another to despotism.

Such was the state of Athens when Theseus succeeded his father Egeas as its sovereign. Of his previous career it is unnecessary to treat here. He lived in an age which was distinguished by the chivalric spirit and personal achievements of individuals, among whom he had acquired great distinction, and it is conceded that he sought consideration and fame in his new and exalted station, more by useful services and concessions to his fellowmen, his subjects, than by the augmentation of his power at their expense. He made many regulations, the great object of which was to improve the condition of the people by giving them a greater participation in the government. He abolished the authority of the several villages, and drew the whole power into Athens, which he made the metropolis of the state. He vested the legislative power in an assembly of the people, whom he divided into three classes: notables, agriculturalists and artisans, taking from the first the principal magistrates, and committing to them the charge of religious duties, with the interpretation of the laws. He retained to himself, in the character of chief hereditary magistrate, the command of the military force only, with the supervision and execution of the laws. With this arrangement the poor were highly gratified, and the rich, although they were dissatisfied, acquiesced.

The interval between Theseus and Codrus, rather more than three centuries, was marked by no signal event. The government remained essentially in the state in which it was placed by Theseus, although frequent dissensions had taken place between the opposite classes. The death of Codrus formed an interesting epoch. The cause and the manner afford proofs equally of his devotion to his country, of his superstition, and of that of the age. The Athenians were engaged in a war with the Dorians, who inhabited the Peloponnesus, and it being reported that the oracle had declared that the party whose king should be slain would succeed, Codrus voluntarily exposed himself in disguise, and was killed. The Dorians immediately retired, and abandoned the war. On this event the Athenians abolished royalty, on the principle that no human being ought to succeed Codrus. As a substitute to royalty they instituted the office of Archon, which they made hereditary in the family of Codrus, commencing with his son Medon, whom they placed by the side of the throne under the obligation to render an account of his administration to the people. This office passed in regular succession to the descendants of Medon, about three hundred and fifty years, when it was made elective at the expiration of every ten years. About seventy years afterwards another more important change was made in it by increasing the number to nine, and making the election annual.

Two other incidents occurred in the Government of Athens prior to the adoption of the Constitution of Solon, which it is proper to notice. The first was formed by the legislation of Draco, which occurred about sixty years after the change last mentioned; the second by that of Epeminides, which followed after that of Draco about twenty-seven years. The laws of the first were remarkable only for their extreme severity and the indiscriminate character of the punishment, no distinction being made between great and small offenses. Every crime was punished with death. His code was legislative only. It did not touch the government. The laws of the second were confined to religious duties, which he regulated to the satisfaction of the people. He was a pious man from Crete. This last agency preceded the Constitution of Solon a few years only.

So great had become the disorder in Athens at this period that the state was menaced with ruin. The divisions between the contending factions had risen to such a height that they were ready to tear each other to pieces. It might reasonably have been expected, after the village authorities were abolished, and the whole people called into one assembly by Theseus, and the legislative power vested in them, that they would have controlled the state and regulated its government and laws as they thought fit: and afterwards, when royalty was abolished, and an Archon substituted for a king, and more especially when the number was increased to nine, and their election made annual, it would seem to follow as a necessary consequence that all impediment to their power was removed. Such too would have been the result if the people of Athens had been competent to self-government. The fact, however, was that they were incompetent, and in consequence those changes operated, comparatively, little in their favor. It does not appear that the people had a right to originate, in any stage in those assemblies, any law or other act whatever. It may be inferred that the power was either in the prince or the notables; and if in the prince, that it passed, after the abolition of royalty, to the Archons, and as all offices were secured to the rich, that it always belonged to that class. Hence it would follow that the power of the king was thrown exclusively into their hands by that change, whereby a complete ascendancy was given to them in the government over the poor. All writers agree, ancient and modern, in representing the condition of the poor, at that epoch, as deplorable. So great had become the ascendancy of the rich that creditors sold their debtors as slaves and compelled parents to sell their children.[34] There were three classes in the state in different circumstances and with different views.[35] Those of the mountains who were poor, sought democracy; those of the plain, who were rich, aristocracy; and those of the coast, who held the middle ground between the two extremes, a mixed government. The poor demanded the abolition of debts and the equal division of lands, which the rich opposed with the utmost violence. They were at the edge of war and no prospect of accommodation by arrangement between themselves. In this state an appeal was made to Solon, and a power granted to him, by common consent, to institute a government for them.

It is proper to remark that in giving a sketch of the government of the ancient republics, it is impossible to do it with that precision which may be observed in describing the Government of the United States or of any of the individual States. In the latter, in both instances, the departments of the government, legislative, executive, and judicial, are so distinctly separated from each other, and the powers of each so well defined, that they may be delineated with the greatest accuracy. Each of those governments is an object, well proportioned in all its parts, standing fully before you. Whereas, in the former, powers different in their nature, and properly belonging to separate and independent branches, are so involved and mixed together, vested in and exercised by the same body, that it is difficult to ascertain what was the precise extent or limit of the powers of any branch, or the true features and character of the government in those very important circumstances. This difficulty is seriously felt in giving a sketch of the

---

[34]Plutarch, Vol. II. page 29. Life of Solon.
[35]*Ibid.* page 28.

Constitution of Solon. The great outline may be taken from the works of Aristotle and Plutarch, and particularly the latter. But other writers have given details, which, under certain circumstances, affect the powers of each branch, whence I have not been able to decide whether they formed a part of the preceding government, originated with him, or were introduced by some of the changes that were afterward made in it. Much light has been shed on the subject by Mr. Berthelemy, the very able author of the work entitled "Anacharsis," but yet he has not entirely removed the difficulty. My object is to present the Constitution in its best form, and to found my remarks on it in that state, and in doing this to render full justice to Solon: to withhold from him nothing to which he was justly entitled; to ascribe to him nothing which was not strictly his own.

Solon did not enter on the discharge of the duties of the high trust committed to him, by commencing with its primary object, the institution of the government. His attention was drawn in the first instance to those of a different character. He met the complaints of the contending parties by a compromise, by which he afforded to each such accommodation as he thought would secure the peace of the state. He refused to make a division of lands, but abolished the debts of individuals.[36] He prohibited also the sale of any citizen for the payment of debts. He repealed some of the laws of Draco and modified others. These facts are mentioned as evidence of the nature of the power which was vested in Solon, whereby that of making laws and instituting a government were confounded together. He was called Legislator, which shows that no nice distinction was then taken between a constitution and a law.

The government which he instituted consisted of an Assembly of the People and a Senate; of a corps of tribunals or Courts of Justice; of a corps of Archons or Magistrates, and of the Senate of Areopagus. These were the only bodies whose powers gave a character to the government. By a strict examination of the organization and endowment of each, we shall be enabled to form a correct judgment of its merits.

The Assembly of the People consisted of the whole body of the people,[37] every citizen above the age of twenty having a right to a seat in it, and no qualification of property being necessary. This assembly had the power, under the restraint which will be noticed, to declare war, to make peace, to receive ambassadors, make treaties of alliance, adopt and repeal laws, establish imposts, appoint all the principal officers of the state, to reward

---

[36]Plutarch, Vol. II. page 36. Life of Solon. Gilliss, Vol. II. page 108.

[37]Aristotle on the Science of Government, Vol. I. Book 2d, ch. 10. Plutarch, Life of Solon, page 88.

merit, and in short perform all the great acts of the government. Six thousand votes were necessary to the passage of its most important acts, and it was a fundamental principle that that number should be present to constitute an assembly. These powers, however, were not absolute. This assembly could originate no proposition whatever: it could decide on none nor act on any but those which were submitted to it by the senate.

The senate consisted of four hundred members, who were appointed in the following manner: The Republic of Athens comprised within its limits a territory of little more than thirty miles square. The whole population of the state was divided into four tribes, each of which sent annually one hundred members to that body. Rather more than eighty years afterward, on the expulsion of the Pisistratides, the number of the tribes was increased to ten by Clisthenes, and the senate to five hundred, each tribe numbering fifty. They were drawn by lot.[38] This body could adopt no act by its own authority. It formed a complete check on the Assembly of the People since the latter could take up none which had not been discussed, approved, and submitted to it by the senate.[39]

As every important measure depended on the sanction of the General Assembly of the People, frequent meetings were indispensable. It was provided therefore by the Constitution, that it should meet for the discharge of its ordinary duties four times in every thirty-five or thirty-six days, the precise day of meeting being adapted to the organization and arrangements of the senate. To each meeting special duties were assigned by a distribution between them of the subjects on which the assembly had a right to act. In the first they confirmed or rejected the magistrates who were to enter into office, examined the condition of the garrisons, heard denunciations, and published an account of the confiscations which had been decreed by the tribunals. In the second they heard the discourses of every citizen who thought proper to address them on public affairs. In the third they received ambassadors who had been presented to the senate. In the fourth they attended to concerns of a pious nature, such as holy feasts and sacrifices.

Extraordinary assemblies were convened whenever a public emergency required it. On these occasions, and especially when the state was menaced with invasion, it was expected that the whole body of the people would attend.

On the first meeting of the senate, after every new election, it was divided into ten classes, each of which in succession took the lead in public

---

[38]Anacharsis, Vol. II. page 274.
[39]Plutarch: Life of Solon, page 42.

affairs for an equal term, the priority being decided by lot. This class was entertained at the public expense at a place called Prytaneum, and was from that circumstance called the Prytanus. It was subdivided into five others, the members of each of which were called Presidents. Special duties were assigned to each in succession. The one in service presided in the senate one day and performed the usual duties of that station. He also held the seal of the republic, the keys of the capitol and of the treasury for that day.

The nine other classes of the senate had also each at its head a President, who was changed at every meeting of the class, and the successor drawn by lot by the chief of the Prytanus. These presidents carried occasionally the decrees of the senate to the assembly of the people, and the chief among them took their votes. On other occasions the chief of the Prytanus, or one of his assistants, performed that office. The Prytanus convened the senate and prepared subjects for its deliberation. As the senate represented the tribes, the Prytanus represented in turn the senate. It was the duty of that class to watch over the dangers to the republic and to warn the senate of any menacing circumstance. The chiefs of the senate presided in the assembly of the people, and when important subjects were agitated, the whole body attended.

These assemblies had not the power in themselves to repeal an ancient law or to pass a new one. Very extraordinary restraints were imposed on them, and forms were prescribed for the exercise of the power vested in them in every instance. The right to submit propositions to the consideration of the senate was not confined to the members of that body. Any citizen might propose to it the repeal of an ancient law if he presented at the same time a substitute for it. If the senate approved the proposition it was communicated to the assembly of the people, and to that meeting which was charged with the examination of the existing laws, which met on the eleventh day of the first month in each year. If it should appear to this assembly that the law ought to be repealed, the Prytanus sent the project to the assembly, which met nineteen days afterwards, and in the meantime published it for the consideration of the people. Five orators were then appointed to attend the assembly to defend before it the law which was attacked. Even this assembly could not decide the question. It appointed Commissioners or Legislators, sometimes one thousand and one, who were united with the Court of Keliastes, the nature of which will hereafter be explained, and who thus united formed a tribunal before which those who attacked and those who defended the law appeared and performed their respective duties. This tribunal might repeal the old law without referring it back to the assembly of the people. They then examined the substitute proposed, and if they approved it, might either confirm it themselves or submit it to the General Assembly of the People.

Such were the powers of the General Assembly of the People and of the Senate with the organization of each body and mode of communication between them. Attention is now due to the other bodies which formed a part of this government, and in the first instance to that of the tribunals or courts of justice which on a well-digested principle is the next in order.

Of these tribunals there were ten, most of which consisted of five hundred judges, and some of a greater number. The judges of these courts were drawn by lot annually by the Archons from the body of the people. No qualification of property was required for either Court. Four of them had jurisdiction of the crime of murder under the classification of accidental, self-defense, etc. No regular time was fixed for the meeting of these courts. The Archons had the power to convene them when in their judgment the duties of the department required it. As the judicial assemblies, for such with great propriety they might be called, were taken from the body of the people and formed a large portion of the same persons who constituted the general assemblies of the people, it was necessary that their meetings should not interfere with each other, and to prevent which interfence power was given to the Archons to fix the time of their meeting.

Of these ten tribunals that of the Keliastes was the most distinguished. It consisted usually of five hundred judges, but on great occasions by the reunion of the other tribunals by order of the Archons the number amounted to six thousand. These judges took the oath to be governed in their decisions by the laws and decrees of the senate and people—to be impartial—to accept no present, and to support the government in its then form.

The delays and expenses of attending trials before these courts induced many to submit their cases to arbitration, and for which, the necessity being anticipated, provision was made by the constitution.

The corps of Archons consisted of nine members, who were elected annually by the people, who assembled on the last four days of each year for the purpose. Any citizen who had borne arms in defense of his country, who had the requisite qualification in property, and who enjoyed a fair reputation by the test of a strict examination in the form prescribed, might be elected to this office. It was the duty of these officers to preserve order in the city and to receive in the first instance public denunciations and the complaints of the oppressed. The first three formed each a special tribunal, in which two assessors chosen by the person himself assisted. The six others called Thermothetes formed a single tribunal only. To these tribunals different causes were assigned. The first was charged with the concerns of widows and orphans. The second with the protection of religious ceremonies from violation. The third with the supervision of foreigners in the city. The last consisting of the six other members fixed the days on which the Superior Courts should hold their sessions, and formed a police for the preservation of order in the city. The Archons who formed Courts carried to the proper tribunals the causes of which they had respectively cognizance, and presided in the trial.

The people elected at the same time with the Archons the generals of the army, infantry and cavalry; those who were charged with the receipt and safe-keeping of the public money; with the supply of the city; with the repair of the public roads; and with other duties of less importance. A chamber of accounts, composed of ten officers, was also chosen every year, and to whom the Archons, the members of the senate, the commanders of the gallies, ambassadors, ministers of the altars, and all others employed in the administration were bound to render an account of the sums which they had received, and of the disbursement thereof.

For the senate and these officers a qualification of property was required in those who held them, and with that view he divided the citizens into four classes, the first of which consisted of those who owned property worth annually five hundred measures of grain or oil; the second three hundred; the third two hundred; the fourth of all others whose property was of less value than the sum last mentioned, which latter were excluded from every office.

The senate of Areopagus was likewise incorporated into this government by Solon. The office was for life. The Archons after their term of service had expired, who could prove that they had discharged the duties of that trust with integrity, became members of that body. They were censors over the public morals; had charge of almost every crime: homicide, arson, poisoning, theft, debauchery, and likewise of innovations in the government and religion.

Such was the government of Athens as instituted by Solon according to the view which I have taken of it from the works of the most enlightened authors, ancient and modern. It will, I am persuaded, be found that no material feature has been omitted or misrepresented. Such likewise was the state of society in which that people were when that government was instituted. On this subject, therefore, in both views I shall make the remarks in execution of the work I have undertaken, which appear to me to be proper.

It will I think be easy to show that this government was altogether an impracticable one; that no government thus organized and endowed could manage the concerns of a state, however small it might be, and that disorder, convulsion, and its overthrow were inevitable. It will be equally easy to show that although the government was strictly democratical, the whole arrangement was in many important circumstances as inconsistent with principle as it was with policy. As this government has been referred to by all writers on the subject of government through the whole intermediate space since its adoption, comprising upwards of two thousand four hundred years, as furnishing the best model of this class, it will be proper to state fully the objections which occur to it. Its fate has been urged as a proof that no government founded on the sovereignty of the people can be sustained. It will be seen on the contrary that so numerous and vital were its defects, that no inference whatever unfavorable to our system can with propriety be drawn from it. I shall nevertheless be as concise as possible, for so glaring and obvious were its defects, that the mere development which has been given of its parts might be sufficient for my fellow-citizens aided as they are by the light of our experience.

In forming a just estimate of the merits of this government we must first decide to what class it belonged. That being fixed, the organization and distribution of its powers will next claim attention.

That the sovereignty was in the people cannot, it is presumed, be controverted. That there was but one order in the government, that of the people. The whole power was vested in them. The senate had no pretension to any right distinct from the people. The members were elected annually, and by lot. The Archons had none, nor had the Areopagus. The first were elected annually, and the second derived their appointment from election, the Archons becoming such after their term of service had expired. The qualification in property required for the senators and other officers did not affect the case, because any citizen who acquired it was eligible, and such changes from the one to the other state in every community are unceasing. The poor acquire property and become rich, and the rich lose it.

To the latter objects, the organization and endowments of the government, my attention will now be directed. By a like view of the above sketch it will be seen that the government was united with the sovereignty. All the great powers of the government were vested in a General Assembly of the People consisting of the whole male population of the state, or otherwise so concentrated in and exercised by them as to produce the same result. The mere enumeration which has been given of the powers vested in that Assembly shows that all those which were legislative and executive belonged to it; and from a view of the organization of the courts of justice and manner of electing the judges, it is equally manifest that although the people who composed them met at other times and at another place, they were members of and formed a large portion of that Assembly, and as may be inferred, sometimes the whole; and in consequence that the judicial power was as much vested in it as if it had been done in express terms. A check was formed by the senate on the exercise of these powers, but it was of a nature to affect only the manner of exercising them, and not the deposit or right of the Assembly to the powers themselves.

As these two features, the exercise of the government by the whole male population of the state, and the union by means thereof of the government with the sovereignty, gave the character to and essentially formed the government, I shall state the objections which occur to each in the first instance, and then proceed with a like view to the other branches. As I consider the defects in these two circumstances radical, it will become an object of inquiry in the analysis of the other branches, whether they were so formed as to mitigate in any degree the evils incident to those defects or to give them greater force. That they produced the latter effect is according to my judgment certain.

When we hear that the General Assembly of the People consisted of the whole male population of the state, and that the attendance of six thousand persons was requisite to form a meeting, the conviction is prompt that the government was altogether impracticable. The number alone would have that effect. We have all seen collections of this kind, and know from experience how incapable they are of discharging the duties of any branch of a government, and how much more so they would be to discharge those of every branch in all its concerns, foreign and domestic. It would be impossible to preserve order in such an assembly in the discussion of the subjects brought before it, without subjecting it to a kind of military discipline, which would be incompatible with its rights. And if order could be preserved all the members could not hear the debate nor understand the merits of the subject under consideration. If all spoke during the meeting, or a large proportion of them, the session would be endless. No rule could be enforced without a vote of the majority, and to ascertain that in a single instance much time would be consumed. On certain occasions and for special objects numerous assemblies of the people have a very useful effect. When serious dangers menace the republic, or great emergencies of any kind occur, it is natural and proper for the people to meet together and declare their sentiments respecting them. From such declaration the government may derive advantage, because it shows the support which may be calculated on if the course designated be pursued. But even on such occasions the debate must be managed by a few, or the proceeding would be marked with clamor, disorder and violence.

Other objections occur to the practicability of a government vested in such numerous assemblies, which are equally decisive. The people at large cannot spare the time, however limited the territory, which a proper discharge of its duties will require. Their private concerns in the various occupations in which they are engaged, with the care of their families, forbid it unless an adequate compensation is allowed for the service. Whence could this be drawn? The revenue of a state is derived from the profits of labor, and if there be no labor there can be no profits. If a trifling compensation be allowed, none but the poor would accept it, and those in the most wretched state, and thus the government would be thrown into the hands of those least competent to it, the consequence of which would be fatal.

I consider this feature alone, the number of which the General Assembly was composed, as decisive against this constitution. No government consisting of such a number can be practicable. Its failure, had there been no other objection to it was inevitable, and the only cause for surprise is that it was not instantaneous.

The objections which apply on principle to the union of the government with the sovereignty are equally strong. When the government is united with the sovereignty there can be no checks whatever on the government. All its acts being those of the sovereign power as well as of the government are conclusive. It is the sovereign power alone that can form such check, and when it is vested in those who hold the government and exercise its powers all check is gone. The party who acts in the government and exercises its powers is responsible to no one for his conduct. There is no superior to call him to account. Each individual holds an equal portion of the sovereignty, as well as of the government, and if he votes with the majority and carries the measure proposed, he has both the constitution and the law on his side be its character what it may. If in the minority and he is dissatisfied, and shows it, the worst consequences may ensue.

When these two powers are united in the people there can be no regular division of power into three branches distinct and independent of each other. The whole will be in one body, that is, in the General Assembly of the People, who will control every measure of every department. Thus all the powers of government, legislative, executive and judicial, will be concentrated in the same body, a concentration which all political writers agree is despotic, and which experience has shown is not less so when united in the people, by the abuses inseparable from it than in one individual, and for a reason which must strike the common sense of all mankind, that in the latter instance the individual when his acts are oppressive will have the whole people against him; whereas in the other the majority will stand together and support each other. If a diversity of interests exist, from whatever cause proceeding, the majority will look to its own, and make laws subservient to it. If differences had occurred and much acrimony been excited, as often happens and from a variety of causes, the oppression of the minority would be certain. Every citizen of the state is not competent to the discharge of the duties of its highest offices, or of any office whatever. Many are unfit for other reasons than the mere want of suitable qualifications. To commit to the unlettered, ignorant, and vicious, trusts whose duties require the highest talents and greatest virtue, would be to sacrifice the interests of the community, to abandon all respect for principle or character. Unite the sovereignty with the government, and deprive the latter of all check in an Assembly whose power would be absolute and uncontrolled, and the overthrow of the government would be inevitable. It has already been shown that such large masses were by their number alone incompetent to the duties of any branch of a government, even that which required the greatest number. When these other objections are duly considered, what must be the conclusion? It must be obvious that such an assembly could not act or think for itself; that the majority would yield to a leader who by subserving their purposes had acquired their confidence, and who at a favorable moment would make use of them for the accomplishment of his own purposes.

Such are the objections which occur to these two features in this government; the number of persons of which the General Assembly was composed, and the union of the government with the sovereignty. I will now state those which apply to the other branches, and first to the Senate.

The Senate had the right, as had been shown, to originate every proposition on which the General Assembly could act. Its powers were therefore commensurate in that respect with those of that Assembly. To form a just estimate of the competency of this body to fulfil the purposes intended by it, we must take into view not only the nature and extent of its powers with its organization, but the relation which it bore to the other branch, the General Assembly of the People. The one consisted of the whole male population of the state in whom the sovereignty was vested; the other of four hundred, who were elected by the tribes by lot. This arrangement, according to every idea which we have formed of the organization of Democratical Government was utterly repugnant to principle. The powers of the Senate comprised every interest within the scope of the legislative and executive departments. Examine its competency in reference to the duties of either, and how will it bear the test? When the legislature of such a government is formed into two branches, the right to originate all laws and other measures within the limit of its powers is invariably committed to the most popular one, and if restraint is imposed on either, it is always on the less numerous. The reason for it is much stronger when that branch is composed of the people themselves. To institute a government on that principle and in that form, and to enjoin on the people to whom the sovereignty belonged, silence, until they heard from another body, would be to announce to them that they were incompetent to the duties assigned to them, and were called there merely as instruments in the hands of such body. From such an arrangement discontent and disorder would be sure to ensue. It might be expected that at every meeting the people would break through such restraint and take the power into their own hands, or that in some other manner the government would be dissolved.

The number of which the Senate consisted was too great for any of the duties assigned to it. It was too great for the popular branch of the legislature of such a state. I may add that it was sufficient for that branch of the legislature of any state, however great its population or extent of territory may be. How utterly incompetent then must it have been for the management of the duties assigned to it, and especially those of an executive nature.

By dividing the Senate into ten classes each of equal number, and giving to each in succession during its term of service thirty-five or thirty-six days, the right to propose subjects for the deliberation of the body, and to take the lead in its affairs in all other concerns, the object undoubtedly was to give greater activity and efficiency to the whole body in the discharge of all its duties. The arrangement, however, could not fail to defeat the object. By permitting the class in service called the Prytanean Corps, to serve for thirty-five or thirty-six days only, and to be succeeded by a like number for a like term, and so on by the others until the whole number had had their turn, and the year expired, would render it impossible for any of them to acquire the knowledge necessary for the discharge of any of the duties. That a provision should have been made by the constitution for a division of the Senate into classes, with the assignment of duties to each class, seems strange. If extensive powers are given to any branch or department of a government of whatever nature they may be, the more that branch is left at liberty to devise the means of carrying them into effect, and the more complete its control over those by whom the duty must be performed, in the selection of proper agents, and supervision of their conduct, especially if of its own members, the better will be the prospect of success, and the greater the responsibility of both parties in the case of failure, to the proper head. By the arrangement made these advantages were lost, for by making the class consist of the precise number which each tribe sent to the Senate, and as may be presumed, of the very members thereof, it would seem as if the government of that body was more a government of the tribes, each in succession, than of a Senate of the Republic, the ill effect of which may easily be conceived.

The mode of proceeding in the passage of laws is a feature in this government of a singular character. The forms to be observed were so complicated, and the bodies to whom the bills or projects were to be submitted, so numerous and different from the ordinary course of legislation, as were the persons who had the right to present such projects, that it seems difficult to form any just estimate of the real objects of the legislator. That which I have formed from a view of the whole subject is, that he intended for the term specified to shut the door against all change of every kind. By giving to any and every citizen the right to present to the Senate a proposition for the adoption or repeal of a law, every citizen was for that great purpose placed on the same footing with the members of that house, and in consequence the obligation on the members and on the body generally, to supervise the police of the state in the operation of the laws, as to their merit or defect was diminished if not entirely annulled. By opening the door thus wide to improvement, it might be inferred at first view that great encouragement and facility had been given to it. But the effect could not well fail to be otherwise. It is a maxim which we often hear repeated in the common concerns of life, that what is the business of every one is that of no one: a maxim which I think is founded in reason, and particularly applicable to the present case. The subsequent process was calculated to produce the same effect, as neither the Assembly of the People, or Senate, in their character as such, were by the ordinary rules and principles applicable to legislative bodies responsible for the final decision, either by the adoption or rejection of the project, they could feel in that capacity little solicitude respecting it. The trial to which the author of the project was subjected, and the punishment which might be inflicted on him if the decision should be adverse to its policy, could not fail to damp the zeal of all parties, as to any change so far, at least, as to take the responsibility on themselves, let the state of affairs be what it might.

If we ask the motive for those restraints, the following occurs: the sovereignty being the people, and they constituting also the government, and having in consequence the right to alter the constitution as well as the laws, it was deemed indispensable to preserve the constitution, to oppose almost insurmountable obstacles to the passage of laws. It is obvious that Solon had no confidence in the capacity of the General Assembly of the People to perform the duties assigned to it, and that he also thought if he did not restrain it from making any change whatever, that the constitution which he had formed would be of short duration. He preferred the Democratical principle; but in instituting the government on that principle, although he did it in the most popular form that could be devised, by vesting all the great powers of the government in the people and making them act in the discharge of those powers collectively, he subjected them in the mode prescribed to such restraints as made them passive rather than active agents in it. It was doubtless for this reason, that the right to originate propositions was inhibited to the Assembly of the People, and vested in the Senate, and for the same reason that it was vested in a company or class of that body, rather than in the body at large.

The judiciary is the branch which claims attention next in the order stated, and which it will be found merits the remarks already made respecting it. It had a species of organization, but not such as to make it an independent corps distinct from the General Assembly of the People. It formed a portion of that Assembly, and often as may be fairly concluded a great majority, if not the whole. It consisted of ten courts composed, each generally of five hundred judges who were chosen by lot from the body of the people, and some of them, particularly that of the the Keliastes, on important occasions of six thousand. The concentration, therefore, of the judicial with the legislative and executive powers in the General Assembly of the People was complete. The objections which apply to the organization in other respects are equally decisive. The sentiment is universal that justice cannot be rendered unless those who administer it possess a thorough knowledge of the law as it is; that such knowledge can be acquired only by long study and practice in the discharge of professional duties. Numerous assemblies can never form wise and safe judicial tribunals. They can neither possess the requisite knowledge of the law, nor be capable of that calm deliberation which is so necessary to a proper discharge of the duties of the trust. Strong appeals will be made in every important case and at every meeting by skillful orators, to their feelings under the influence of which their decision will often be rendered without regard to principle, and in direct opposition to judgments previously rendered in similar cases. Experience has shown that even for the most extensive and populous communities the courts of justice should consist of a few members only, who should be selected from the whole society for their talents and virtues, and particularly those which qualify them for the office. They should likewise hold office during good behaviour, or at least so long as they were able to discharge the duties. When courts are thus organized and composed of such men they are entitled to, and command the confidence of the nation. Their decisions stand together and form a consistent and compact system which all approve. The judges are detached from and unconnected with local and political circles. They have no points to carry, nor motive in the sense in which it is generally understood to court popular favor. They represent the nation of whom they take nothing but its good opinion, founded on the rectitude and wisdom of their decisions.

By the powers vested in the corps of Archons, it appears that they were altogether of a character judicial and ministerial. This corps had long formed, as has been shown, a part of the existing government of that people. It had been substituted for monarchy and was connected with the idea of liberty, and preserved as may fairly be inferred, more in accommodation with the prejudices of the people than for any other cause. When so many courts of justice were instituted, it cannot but excite surprise that he should have taken from them any portion of the judicial power and committed it to this corps. The other power vested in it might likewise have been otherwise easily disposed of. It is obvious that by preserving the corps, he made the government more complicated and difficult of action.

The same remarks are applicable to the Senate or Court of Areopagus. This court had been instituted in the early age of the republic, at which period it formed a species of council to the King and of court for the community. All the power given to it was so much taken from the king, and a step in the degree towards popular government. This corps was therefore cherished by the people in every stage, and the more so because being composed of their most enlightened and best citizens of advanced age it merited their confidence. Solon found it necessary to preserve it, and in so doing to invest it with such powers as would make it instrumental, according to his view of the subject, to the general purposes of his constitution. It had held from its origin judicial powers. By committing to it those of that nature he made no change in principle, although he made the government more complicated. A censorship over the public morals seemed to fall within that scope, as judges generally have that kind of power. In what manner the charge given to it over innovations in government and religion was to be exercised does not appear. The court could not, as is presumed, declare a law to be void as unconstitutional, because so numerous and great were the obstacles to the passage of any law, that such a proposition would have been useless. I consider the power as monitory only in both instances. He retained the corps for the same reason that he did the Archons. To have abolished it would have shocked the public feeling, and in retaining it he was compelled to carve out for it a sphere of action in the discharge of the duties whereof if it rendered no important service, it might do little harm.

From this view of the government of Athens I think it may fairly be concluded, by the numbers of which it was composed in every department, had there been no other objection to it, that it was an impracticable one. I think also the conclusion equally obvious that the organization and endowment of its parts being repugnant to principle, were in themselves by the abuses inseparable from them sufficient to overthrow it. These causes united could not fail at an early day to produce that result. The best commentary, however, on that government is its career and fate, of which I will now give a short sketch.

It was the intention of Solon that it should be binding on the people one hundred years without any change, on the presumption, as is inferred, that if it remained in force that term the power would be permanently established in the people; and in case it should appear that any modification of it suited them better, they would acquire in the interval sufficient knowledge of the science of government to enable them to amend it without exposing themselves to any danger. All the public officers and the people bound themselves by an oath to support it as soon as it was reported. The Constitution and laws were then inscribed on rolls of wood and posted in the citadel and other public places for the inspection of the people. Immediately after the publication he was beset by persons of every class who were dissatisfied, to make amendments of it, some in one form and some in another, until, to rid himself of the annoyance, he resolved to leave the country and to remain abroad ten years, which purpose he executed. Before his departure he obtained an oath from the whole community to preserve it during his absence. On his return at the expiration of that term he found that the factions had revived with great violence, and that affairs had relapsed nearly into the same state in which they were before his government was adopted. An incident occurred soon after his return and in his presence which showed that his government had no adhesive quality or efficiency: that it was a cobweb. Pisistratus, a descendant of one of their ancient kings, a man of fortune, had to serve his own purposes become a leader of the poor, who formed the most numerous class. He fomented the discontent between the factions and exposed himself by his violence to the hatred of the rich. Seizing a favorable occasion he inflicted his body with wounds and rushed into the streets covered with blood, declaring that his enemies, who were the enemies of the people, had made an attempt on his life, and calling on them to defend him as the best means of defending themselves. The Assembly of the People and Senate were immediately convened and a guard granted to him, of which he soon afterwards availed himself, to take possession of the citadel and usurp the government. In this emergency Solon sustained his character for integrity and devotion to the rights of the people. He opposed the usurpation and exposed the fraud by which it was attempted, but without effect. The people were deceived and made the instrument of their own depression by an ambitious and unprincipled intriguer.[40]

Pisistratus lived thirty-three years after his usurpation, of which he reigned seventeen. Twice he was deposed and as often recovered the power of which he died possessed, transmitting it to his sons, Hippias and Hipprachus. The latter was killed by Harmodius and Aristogiton in revenge for a personal injury. Hippias maintained his authority a few years but was at length overthrown, principally by the exertions of Clisthenes, chief of the Alemaeonides, with the aid of Lacedemon. The usurpation of Pisistratus was of a peculiar character. It marked the rude state of the people and their incapacity for self-government, as it likewise did the dexterity with which the usurper availed himself of the good qualities as well as the weaknesses to accomplish the object of his unprincipled ambition. He did not assume the title of king, nor admit that he had subverted the constitution of Solon. He assumed only the title of magistrate or perpetual chief of the state, under which he exercised his usurped powers to what extent he pleased. He left to the government of Solon all its forms, but deprived it of all its force. He preserved the General Assembly of the People and Senate, and maintained the laws in their ordinary operation, by means whereof he secured to his own government the character of Democracy, while he ruled every department with absolute sway. His sons followed his example, but not with the same success. Hippias when expelled found a refuge in Persia, where he joined the army of Darius and was slain in the battle of Marathon fighting against his country.

The power wrested from Hippias passed over to Clisthenes, the leader of the party by whom he was overthrown. It was natural and accorded with principle that it should have returned to the people, but they were not competent to the exercise of it. He is represented to have been governed by patriotic motives and to have been a friend of liberty. He restored the constitution of Solon with some changes which do not appear to have touched the principle of the government. He increased the number of the tribes to ten, and of the Senate to five hundred, and of the officers who formed the board of accounts in like degree.

From the overthrow and expulsion of Hippias, to the subjugation of Greece by the armies of Rome under the Consul Mummius, about three hundred and sixty-four years intervened. The improvement of the people in civilization in that interval was considerable, and grew out of causes natural and obvious. Their progress in agriculture, navigation, commerce and the arts, called for an augmented population and furnished the means

---

[40]Herodotus, Vol. I. page 57.

of supporting it. The variety of pursuit by giving birth to new ideas expanded the human mind. It was in this interval that the States of Greece acquired their greatest renown, and it is of course that portion of their history which has procured for them, in the highest degree, the respect and admiration of all succeeding ages. No one hears mention of the battles of Marathon, Salamis, or Platea; of the voluntary sacrifice of the illustrious band who perished at the Straits of Thermopylae in defense of their country; or of the abandonment of the city of Athens by the whole people when invaded by the overwhelming force of Persia, without experiencing sensations of enthusiastic delight. Characters were then formed in many of the states whose names have been handed down and will never be forgotten, which do honor to the human race. But it is not in this view that the subject on which I treat now claims my attention. How were the people of Athens governed during this interval? Did they maintain the constitution of Solon and administer it strictly according to its principles, or was that constitution set aside and some other substituted for it? If changes occurred, to what cause or causes were they imputable? These are the immediate objects of inquiry, and to which I shall confine myself with the utmost rigor. When it is proved, as it is by the concurrent testimony of all historians that this constitution was overthrown immediately after its adoption by the people who adopted it, and who were bound by an oath to support it, that this was done in the presence of its author, who exerted all his faculties to maintain it, there is little reason to presume that it could be maintained afterwards. Much might fairly be ascribed from the manner in which that event was accomplished, to the rude and unlettered state in which the people then were; but it is nevertheless true that the government was an impracticable one: that it was as ill adapted to the civilized as to the rude state, and the great cause for surprise is that as their improvement in civilization and knowledge of every kind was great, they did not in their progress, when they had the power in their hands, amend their government in such a manner as to give it a practical and efficient form. From an attentive view of the state of Athens and of Greece through the whole of that interval which is now the object of attention, it would be obvious that many causes united to produce that effect. I will notice the two principal only. The first relates to the epoch in which that government was instituted. The second to the state of Greece generally in the relation which was preserved between that people as a power and other nations, and likewise between the states themselves.

It has been shown that when the government belonged exclusively to the people they exercised its great powers collectively or en masse, and that when it was decided between different orders, of which they formed one, they always exercised their portion in the same manner. Such was then the state of society and of the science growing out of it that to part from the power, and place it in other hands, of representatives for example, would have been regarded by them as the abandonment of it. The contest which took place between the people and the prince in the several states after the societies had increased and the claim to hereditary right was set up, always involved the question whether the people should exercise the power in that mode or be governed absolutely by him, and it was the impracticability of the government when they got possession of it that soon overthrew it. An amendment, therefore, by committing their power to representatives was, it is presumed, not even thought of. They nevertheless still retained their attachment and devotion to liberty, of which they gave unceasing and very strong proofs.

The other cause alluded to formed likewise a very serious obstacle. Almost the whole of this interval was employed in wars, foreign and internal or civil. The first commenced with Persia shortly after the expulsion of the Pisistratide, and lasted with some intermissions fifty-one years. The Peloponnesian war followed soon afterward and consumed almost an equal term. This war commenced between Athens and Lacedemon, but all the other states soon became parties to it as allies on the one or the other side. It was produced by the war with Persia and by the rivalship and jealously which were excited in that war between those two states. To this war the ruin of Greece may in a great measure be ascribed, since it formed a relation between the states which had a very injurious influence on their respective governments, and also on the bond by which they were then held together. Other wars ensued, among which that between Sparta and Messenia was the most durable and destructive. That between Athens and Syracuse was the next, which shook the foundation of the Athenian state. The war between Sparta and Thebes followed, the fortune of which raised the latter from a very inferior to a very distinguished rank among the states of Greece. Other wars occurred between the states which did great injury to the local as well as the general interest, of which that between Martena and Tigra, to which almost all the states became parties, had the most pernicious effect. Such continual warfare could not fail to check their growth, to prevent all improvement in their local governments, and to weaken and almost annihilate the federal bond.

Under such circumstances it was easy for a power, even of inferior population, whose force should be united and directed against them with energy and talent to overwhelm them. Macedon presented such a power with a leader who was capable and eager to profit by these divisions between the states and to raise himself at their expense. Until then Macedon had been little known. She had made no impression on the affairs of Greece, and been dependent on some of the states, Sparta and Athens, at different intervals for protection. Her rise was owing altogether to the talent of Philip, who under various pretexts made war first on one state and then on the others, until finally he succeeded in reducing all under his dominion. From this period the affairs of Greece became connected with those of Macedon, and incidentially with the fortune of her rulers in their enterprises in Asia. Philip did not treat Greece in all respects as a conquered territory. He left each state in the enjoyment of its own government, and added but little from the dominions of either to his own. He became a member of the Amphyctionic Council, placed himself at its head and controlled its measures. His great object was a war with Persia, to which he was tempted by her wealth and a confidence in success arising from the repeated defeat of her vast armies in the recent invasions of Greece, by the comparatively small force of the Grecian states. Under his influence the Amphyctionic Council declared war against Persia, and committed the management of it to him in the character of commander-in-chief of the forces employed in the expedition.

His sudden death by assassination suspended this war, but his son Alexander who succeeded him, and who with equal if not superior talents adopted his policy, soon renewed the war and prosecuted it with great ardor and unexampled success. The death of Philip excited a hope in the Grecian states that they might extricate themselves from the Macedonian yoke, but that was transitory. In one year it was fixed more firmly on them by Alexander than it had been by his father. Of his conquests in Asia and of the disorders and revolutions produced by his death, by the contests between his lieutenants for portions of the conquered dominions to which they respectively set up their pretensions, I shall not treat. Little change was wrought thereby in the affairs of Greece. New efforts were made by several of the states to recover their liberties, which were attended with various success. The revival of the Ochaien League with its efforts in defense of that cause forms an interesting epoch in the latter stage of those republics. In Athens the Democracy was occasionally subverted and restored, but no change in the form ever attempted. Such was the train of events which occurred in the interval specified, and such the state of Athens at its termination, which was marked by the subjugation of Greece and her rendition to a Roman province.

These causes are, it is presumed, sufficient to show why the people of Athens never improved the constitution of Solon at any time during their existence as an independent state. The question still remains to be solved, how were they governed when that constitution was declared to be in force? Did the people govern themselves in the only mode which can be regarded as self-government, or were they mere instruments in the hands of individuals in whom they reposed their confidence? That the latter was the fact must be evident to all who examine their history with impartiality and candor. Their confidence was at one time placed in one individual, and at other times in others, who shaped the course pursued and ruled them absolutely while it lasted. The people stood collected in the General Assembly with their eyes fixed on the tribune, from which the orators addressed them, with their minds made up whose counsel to adopt and whose to reject, before they heard the proposition of either. Miltiades, Themistocles, and Aristides, ruled them through a great part of the Persian war; Cimon, Alcibiades, Nicias and Phocion had their turn. Pericles ruled in the Peloponnesian war, and others succeeded on other occasions. No instance can be given in which the people took affairs into their own hands, digested propositions adapted to existing exigencies, debated and amended them as they thought fit, and acted as a government. The constitution forbade it, and had it been otherwise, it would have been impracticable under the existing organization. The individuals who ruled did it altogether by personal influence. It was not by virtue of any office which they held of Senator, Areopagate, Archon and any other. In these offices no such power was vested incompetent to the discharge of its duties, and in consequence while they preserved the form and in truth held the power in their own hands, transferred the actual exercise of it to leaders whose instrument they were.

Confidence is due to exalted talents and merit, and respect to the individual to the extent of that claim; but so soon as the influence of any one citizen becomes a power which undermines and destroys the independence of the people, whether it be wielded by himself or a party, the effect is for the time despotic. Pisistratus usurped the government and exercised its powers in his own right. In the accomplishment of that object the people were his instruments. They were so, because they considered him their friend and the friend of liberty. They thought themselves free, and that in supporting him they defended their own cause. They were deceived. The principle in his case was different from that which existed in the latter instances, but the effect in regard to the agency of the people in the government was essentially the same. The power of the individual while he enjoyed their confidence was absolute, and the loss of it was marked by convulsion. They treated him as a tyrant, and punished him by banishment or death. It was the same with Miltiades, Themistocles, Alcibiades, Aristides and others, that it was with Pisistratus and his son, Hippias. Their most illustrious men either died in prison under fines which they could not pay, or were banished, and perished in foreign countries. The whole body of the people must have the knowledge necessary to make them competent to self-government, and the government must be wisely organized and endowed or it cannot be free or durable.

How happened it then that Solon should have instituted such a government? Data exist to afford the answer. The basis on which his constitution rested, and which could not be changed, furnishes it. It was not his object to take the power from the people and reduce them to slavery, nor could he have done it if he had been so disposed; and if they held any it could only be in a General Assembly of the whole people, the form in which they had held it from the time of Theseus, upwards of eight hundred years. To take it from them in that form would have been viewed in that light. The principle of election and of representation to certain offices and in certain stations was well understood and practiced in several of the Grecian republics, but it was never carried beyond a certain limit. It never touched the great powers, or what might be called the share which the people held in the sovereignty of the state. He was forced, therefore, to preserve that feature in the government. How then accommodate the differences which existed in the community between the rich and the poor, or as may be understood, the class of notables which had been instituted by Theseus, without prostrating the latter? How make an efficient government in any form whatever? If the power of the General Assembly which consisted of a vast majority of the poor was not checked, the accommodation would not have stopped with the abolition of debts. The lands would also have been sold and in all other respects the notables have been prostrated or the government have been overset. How form that check? The Archons could not be made, by any power which might be given to them, a balance against the Assembly of the People. The first of that corps had been instituted to get rid of a king, and the number was afterwards increased on the same principle to abolish all regal power. An attempt to restore the power in that form would have been absurd. Nor could the Court of Areopagus have been made instrumental to such a purpose. It had always been composed of aged men who had filled other offices and retired into that corps as it were from the contentious scene of public life. To vest it in the notables as an hereditary branch would have been impossible, as it would have been sure to have brought on the convulsions and civil war which it was sought to avoid. There seemed, therefore, to be no other resource than to institute a body, which by its numbers, mode of election and weight of character, might stand well with and command the confidence of the General Assembly, and by the qualification required for the members in property and the power vested in that body, forming in like extent a restraint on the General Assembly, should secure the rich from ruin and obtain likewise their confidence. It was on this principle and with this view, as I presume, that the Senate was instituted.

Had the Senators been elected by the whole people in any other mode, by the General Assembly for example, or by a vote of every citizen for every member, the Senate would have been in effect a Committee of the General Assembly, and would have been essentially under its control. By making the members eligible by the tribes, he detached the body in some measure from the General Assembly, and by requiring a certain portion of property as a qualification for the office he gave some security to the rich, while by leaving the door open to all who might acquire it, the objection which would have applied to hereditary rank was precluded, and some hope was presented to the poor. And by giving to the Senate the exclusive power to originate every proposition on which the General Assembly could act he gave an additional protection to the rich. Give to the General Assembly the power to originate measures and no resistance could have been made to it. The rich would have been overwhelmed at once. Confine its agency to propositions which the Senate should submit to it, and that consequence would be avoided. The rich would never propose any act which would operate against themselves. The Senate therefore seemed to be as well adapted to all these objects as any corps which he could have instituted could be. But the government was impracticable in every part, as has been shown by a fair analysis of the organization and endowment of each, when tested by the nature and qualities of man, and likewise by the career and fate of the government itself. For the defects of the system we must look to the age in which it was instituted and to the state of society and of the science in that age. That nothing better could have then been done, the devotion of the people to the government and their observance of its injunctions, so far as they understood and were able to execute them under all their difficulties afford the best proof.

The General Assembly could be preserved only by investing it with the powers committed to it; but in the execution of those powers that it should not act from its own impulse but be the instrument of some other party. To accomplish this it was necessary that it should take that position of its own accord and not by compulsion; that it should believe that it was the ruling party while it was ruled; that it did everything when it did nothing. This was seen in the instance of Pisistratus, and likewise in the others that have been noticed, for although the principle was different the effect was the same. The tendency in all governments, even those which are representative, in which the bodies are too numerous, and in which those who compose them act as the multitude connecting in the degree the sovereignty with the government, is to precipitate their overthrow and termination in one, that is, in despotism. When the sovereignty is held by a prince in the early and rude state of society, and the people in the progress of civilization and increase of population contend for their rights, compromises are natural and are generally entered into. Whatever the people obtain is so much gained, and they are often satisfied with small gains. In the early stages the power of the prince is not despotic. There is always a class of nobles around him who share a portion of the power, and the spirit of equality pervades the whole society, prince, nobles and people. The effort is therefore to improve the condition of the people, and in doing this the hold which the two hereditary branches have acquired though diminished is not always destroyed. But when the people possess the whole power, and a change is made, it is generally by a transition to the opposite extreme. Possessing the whole power and not being able to retain it they lose the whole. There is no resting-place; no point at which to stop; no party with whom to negotiate: and they will never voluntarily degrade themselves by creating a class of nobles with a prince over them, and retain a portion of the power only in the government. Changes in this state generally grow out of contests between rival parties and rival chiefs. Civil wars ensue, in the result of which the leader of the successful party is placed at the head of the government with unlimited power. Our object is to preserve the sovereignty in the people and to give them that agency in the government which will be best adapted to that end, and in those instances in which the agency of a few or of one will be most effectual, to avail ourselves of it, but in a manner which will make them or him perform their duties with fidelity as representatives and servants, without the possibility of their wresting the power from us and becoming our masters.

From the view above presented it is obvious that the Government of Athens had not a single feature in it except the principle on which it was founded, which was free from serious objection; and that its defects were so numerous and vital as to make its overthrow certain and immediate. There was no regular division of power in it; of legislative, executive and judicial, separated from each other. The whole was an amalgamation.

For these evils no remedy can be found but by the separation of the sovereignty from the government, retaining the forms in the people, and committing the latter to representatives to be by them elected or otherwise appointed, deriving their authority from them, and placed in offices or departments organized and endowed by a compact or constitution to which the whole people are parties, and by which their duties in their capacity of the sovereign power and of their representatives in the departments to which they may be called, shall be specially and distinctly defined. If the two powers be thus separated and the government be organized on just principles, divided into the three departments specified with the proper number, and proper powers be vested in each, with a line strictly drawn between them, and each be made independent of the others, and armed with the means of securing that independence by checking encroachments of either on the other, it is impossible that the government should fail, provided the people be competent to self-government and perform their duty. When the sovereign power is separated from the government by a compact to which the whole people are parties, and by which the rights and interests of all are placed on the same footing, all are equally interested in the faithful execution of its conditions according to their true intent and meaning, by a fair and just construction, and are equally bound to enjoin it on those who represent them. In this case the people may form a complete check on the government, and if they be intelligent and virtuous, keep it in its true course. The path for every department will be traced and seen by those in each, in any and every emergency as well as by their constituents. The people who are calm spectators at a distance of the measures pursued and of the conduct of those in office will be guided by principle, and expect a faithful observance of it by those who represent them. Upright and honorable men will always pursue that course, and even those who are less scrupulous, knowing that their conduct is watched will be afraid to go wrong.

LACEDEMON

I WILL now proceed to examine the Government of Lacedemon. The constitution instituted by Lycurgus is that of which I shall treat. It was instituted eight hundred and forty-five years before the Christian era and two hundred and fifty-one before that of Athens. It will be found that this government was in many of its features peculiar: that no such government ever existed either in the ancient or modern world. It affords in all its parts the strongest exemplification of the epoch in which it was formed.

In tracing the origin of the Athenian state with its progress for the purposes of this inquiry, it was necessary to take a concise view of that of all Greece. The view thus presented is equally applicable to Lacedemon. The early or rude ages of all the states are similar. So far as any incidents occurred in the progress of those two communities of a different character, I shall endeavor to notice and give them the weight to which they are entitled.

Their government had a like origin in princes; a form which was common to the Grecian States, and incident to the rude age in which they commenced. A difference occurred in that of Lacedemon, which distinguished it in that respect from every other state. The first prince died, leaving two sons who inherited the office of the father with equal rights, and which descended to the eldest son of each branch through successive generations for many ages.

It has been already observed that Danaus from Egypt, and Pelops from Phrygia, emigrated to the Peloponnesus at a very early age, while the people were in a rude state, and that they were each placed at the head of the section in which they settled. These princes had respectively a long train of descendants who had great power in that Peninsula. The Heraclidae were the offspring of Danaus, so called from Hercules, one of his descendants, the Pelopidae of Pelops. These two houses contended for the supremacy in the Peloponnesus, in which struggle the Pelopidae succeeded, and the Heraclidae were banished from it. This occurred some time before the Trojan war, in which Agamemnon of the house of the Pelopidae took the lead as commander of the confederate force employed in it. The long absence of the chiefs engaged in that war had so far impaired their authority in their respective dominions, that many of them were compelled on their return, to engage in new wars, to reinstate themselves. Agamemnon was betrayed by his wife, and cut off immediately after his return. The Heraclidae, aware of these disorders, and of the favorable opportunity which it presented, made several attempts to regain their power, in which they failed; but at length they succeeded. In the latter they were aided by the Dorians and Etolians. Temenus, Cresphontes, and Aristodemus, three brothers in the fifth degree from Hercules, led the invading force. Almost the whole of the Peninsula was conquered. In the division of the portion claimed by the Heraclidae, Argos was allotted to Temenus, Messinia to Cresphontes, and Laconia to the two twin brothers, Euryelpenes and Procles, the infant sons of Aristodemus, who died pending the struggle. The other conquered provinces were divided between the Dorians and Etolians, who had assisted in making the conquest.

The Heraclidae were thus restored to their possessions in the Peloponnesus about eighty years after the taking of Troy, and one thousand three hundred and five before the Christian era. Two kings were thus placed at that early period in the government of Lacedemon, and in that state Lycurgus found it when he instituted his constitution, four hundred and sixty-eight years afterwards. What were at that period the other modifications of the Lacedemonian government does not distinctly appear in any work that I have seen, ancient or modern. It may be inferred from the remarks of some writers that there existed a class of nobles with limited powers. The power of the kings is said to have been absolute whenever they could agree, but that differences between them were frequent, and sometimes serious; and that these differences laid the foundation of the power held either by the nobles or people. In general it is understood from the view which has been presented by different writers, that the progress of affairs in Lacedemon was similar in other respects to that which occurred in the other states. There were frequent contentions through the whole interval, between the different orders for power, and it may be presumed had not the difference between the two kings, mitigated in the exercise of that which belonged to them, and thereby given a popular cast to the government, that it would have experienced the fate which befell monarchy in all the other states, and been overthrown at the same time. All writers agree that these contentions had risen to a great height at the period when Lycurgus was called on, apparently by the general voice, to institute the government of which I shall give a sketch.

The attention was drawn to him by causes which marked the epoch at which the constitution was formed, as well as the confidence reposed in his virtue and talents. He was the son of Eunomus, and brother of Polydaetes, one of the reigning kings and a descendant of Hercules in the eleventh degree. His brother dying without offspring, he was supposed to be entitled to the crown, and actually did succeed to it for a short term; but it appearing that the deceased king had left his wife pregnant, he disclaimed any right to it, in case the offspring should be male. The widow offered to destroy the infant if he would marry her. He amused her with hope until a son was born, whom he acknowledged, and in whose favor he immediately abdicated. This proof of disinterested virtue elevated his character in the state; but the disappointment and mortification to which the widow was thereby subjected excited her deep resentment, and exposed him to danger. She soon raised factions against him, in consequence whereof he left the state and traveled into Crete, and thence to Asia, studying the laws and governments of different countries, and comparing them with each other as to their relative success in promoting the happiness of people. In his absence Lacedemon was convulsed by factions and the state menaced with dangers, for which no remedy could be found within it. They all united in pressing his return, and in giving him a power to make such reforms as would avert the impending ruin. I shall present this constitution as instituted by him, and notice the changes afterwards made in it while in force. He complied with the invitation and reported the constitution which was established before the Christian era, of which I will now give a sketch, with the changes.

The government of Lacedemon consisted of two kings, of a Council of twenty-eight members, and of an Assembly of the People. The crown was hereditary in both branches, descending to the oldest son of each, and if no son to the brother, or other nearest connection of that branch; but in no event to the other house. Their rights were joint and equal, not divided between them. The senators who composed the Council were elected for life by the people. The election was made in full assembly. The kings presided in the senate. The measures carried there were communicated to the people in General Assembly, who were bound either to accept or reject them without amendment.

When the two kings concurred in any proposition there was no opposition to it. Neither could leave the state in time of peace, nor could both do so in time of war; unless there were two armies in the field, in which case each took the command of one. They were placed at the head of religion, and had the command of the armies, might sign truces, and receive and dismiss ambassadors while in the field. In peace they were regarded only as the first citizens of the state. They mixed in society with the other citizens on a footing of equality, and were received with respect but without parade.

The Senate being the Supreme Council of the state, war and peace, alliances, and all the other high concerns, were treated of in the first instance in it. No person under the age of sixty could be elected to it. In addition to the high political powers already noticed, others of a judicial character belonged to that body. When a king was accused of having betrayed the state, or having violated the laws, the Senate with the other king and five Ephori, after that corps was instituted, formed the tribunal by which he was tried.

Of the Assembly of the People there existed two distinct species. One regulated affairs which were peculiar to the inhabitants of Sparta. The other those which were common to them, and to the inhabitants of the different villages of Laconia. The kings, senators, and different classes of magistrates assisted in both.

When the succession to the throne was regulated, magistrates were chosen or dismissed. The Assembly was composed of Spartans only. This Assembly was convened in the ordinary course of affairs every month at full moon, and at other times when circumstances required it.

The other Assembly was convened when war, peace, or alliances were treated of. It was composed of Spartans, and likewise of deputies from the villages of Laconia, and often of those from their allies, and of nations who came to solicit aid from Lacedemon. In these Assemblies their mutual pretensions and complaints, the infractions of treaties by other people, the means of conciliation, the projects of campaigns, and the contributions they had to furnish, were brought forward and discussed.

Other provisions were introduced into this government of a very peculiar character, which although they do not constitute essentially a part of the organization, or of the endowment of either branch, or touch directly the question of hereditary or popular right, yet as they formed a part of the compact between the people and the kings, and the people themselves, and had great influence on the fortune of the government, it is equally proper to notice. These provisions were the basis on which the system rested, and were in fact a part of the constitution itself. I shall notice the most important only. They mark distinctly the state of society at the age of which I treat.

He made an equal division of all the land among the citizens of the state. He divided Laconia into thirty thousand parts or lots, and distributed them among the people of the country. He divided Sparta into nine thousand, which he distributed in like manner among the people of that section. The proprietors of these lots could neither sell nor divide. They descended to the oldest son of each citizen, and were rather the property of the state than of the individual. He banished gold and silver and substituted iron as the currency, and of such weight and little value that it required a cart and two oxen to carry a piece worth comparatively a few dollars. He expelled the fine arts by prescribing the kind of furniture which should be used, and giving every other possible discouragement to them. He established public repasts, and made all the citizens mess together on the same food, which was regulated by law, of the simplest kind, and dressed in like manner. Each table consisted of fifteen persons, and each person furnished monthly an equal portion of the provisions requisite, which was calculated with great precision. The kings attended these tables, and partook of the public repasts with the citizens without other distinction than the allowance of a double portion to each. From these tables they were obligated to return to their houses in the dark. It was ordained that the laws should not be written, but preserved in the memory alone; and science of every kind was discountenanced except that of war and the exercises connected with it. Marriages, births, and the education of children were specially provided for. Girls were taught to perform manly exercises, to throw the quoit and the javelin, to run the race, and wrestle in public naked. The same instruction was given to boys. The infant as soon as born was inspected by persons appointed for that purpose and taken in charge of the government. If well formed and robust, vigorous nourishment was provided for him, and a lot of land assigned to him. If deformed, delicate and weak, he was thrown into a bog and destroyed. He discouraged all intercourse between the citizens of Sparta and those of other nations by a visit of either to the country of the other, especially in that class whose example could have any effect, from a fear that the morals of the Spartans might thereby be corrupted. His object was to keep them as much as possible at home under the daily influence of the institutions which he had established, and to exclude all extraneous usages which might tend to produce a change.

Such was the government of Lacedemon, as instituted by Lycurgus, and in which state it remained about one hundred and thirty years, in the course of which time the people being dissatisfied with the restraint imposed on them, either to accept or reject the propositions which were sent to them by the senate, without amendment, gradually assumed the right of making such alterations as they thought fit. This abuse, as it was called, was corrected in the reign of Potedorus and Theoporapus, by whom the constitution was restored to its original state. The discontent which that measure produced among the people may easily be conceived. To reconcile them to it, the corps called the Ephori was instituted as a substitute in defense of their rights, and by which a very important change was introduced into the system. I shall make the remarks which appear to me to be proper on this constitution, as originally formed by its author, and then notice the effect which was produced by this change.

The most celebrated writers of antiquity represent this government as one of the best, if not the best, which was instituted at that epoch. Aristotle, Polybius, and Plutarch have explicitly avowed that sentiment, and some modern writers of great merit seem to acquiesce in it. I will examine it on principle, giving full force to every provision in it which could have had any influence on its fortune. I will then test it by its career, since that is the best criterion by which a just estimate can be formed of its merit. With this view, it will be proper to inquire in the first instance to what class did it belong? Did it recognize distinct orders in such extent as to belong strictly to that class, and to move on that principle?

The character of a government must depend on the source from whence it derives its powers. All governments which emanate directly from the people, whether the term of service of those who fill its branches be long or short, are popular or democratical, provided when the term expires the vacancy is supplied by election. The length of the term will vitiate the government, but cannot be said to change the principle although it be for life. It is not the name or title given to any incumbent in any branch which fixes the character of the government. An officer may be called king, and the office may be hereditary in his family, and yet if he has no power, or the power vested in him be very limited, and especially if the people have a control over his conduct, the government cannot be considered as strictly monarchical. For the government to be placed in that class, the person having the title must hold a portion of the sovereignty, otherwise it will be nominal only. This may be done in various forms and in different degrees in different governments, but still in the degree that the control of the great affairs of the state, and especially the power which is generally considered as executive, is taken from him and vested in the people and the office made ministerial, will the principle and character of the government be changed, and an approach be made to democracy.

The power of the kings was very limited. They were chiefs of religion, and commanded the armies in time of war. In the internal government of the state they had no effective power whatever. They were members of and presided in the senate, but their votes were counted like those of other members, and they had in its measures when they disagreed no other weight than what arose from the respect which was due to their talents and merit. They did not receive ambassadors from nor appoint them to foreign powers, nor instruct them when appointed, nor make treaties, nor appoint officers, nor had they any other powers than those above enumerated.

The government of Lacedemon resembled that of Athens in its most important features. The sovereign power was essentially in the people, in the one government as well as in the other, and all the great powers of the government were vested in and exercised by the people collectively in a General Assembly in both. The government was united with the sovereignty, and in consequence the same concentration of legislative, executive and judicial powers existed in the General Assembly of the one state as in that of the other. The material difference between the two governments consisted in the power held by the two kings, in that of Lacedemon and in the hereditary quality of that power; and likewise in the number of members of which their senates respectively were composed, and in their term of service. How far these differences may be considered as forming a difference between the two governments on principle, and introducing distinct orders into that of Lacedemon, and were calculated to produce a difference in their fate, are objects of inquiry which merit attention.

The senators of Lacedemon held their offices for life; those of Athens for one year only. In both states they were elected by the people. The length of service, as has been remarked, will weaken the tone and spirit of the government, but cannot change the principle; nor will it entirely change the principle of action in those who hold the office, for as their offspring will be in the hands of the people the dread of the revenge which might fall on them, would deter the incumbents from committing acts to incur their resentment. The hereditary right of the kings as members of and to preside in the senate, and to command the armies in war, are the only powers over which the people had not a direct control, by the election of those in whom vested; and is, therefore, the only feature in the government of Lacedemon which takes it out of the democratic class.

If a democratical government be so badly formed as to be impracticable, and the people avail themselves of a resource founded on the opposite principle, to sustain it, of very limited extent, and with effect, it can furnish no proof other than the excellence of the democratical principle. It can furnish none of the excellence of that of the opposite character, nor of the comparative merit of democratical government in its best form, with those which are mixed.

When a principle opposite to that on which the government is founded has no hold on the government, and is merely an outward prop or stay on which it rests, under difficulties which admit of obvious remedies, we cannot reason on it as a conflicting power, nor can it afford any proof of the defect of one principle or merit of the other. A drowning man it is said will catch at a straw. He will certainly take the hand of his enemy to save his life. If the opposite principle has such strong hold on the government as to be able to check its progress in case of division, and to endanger its existence in that of conflict, then the question of distinct orders, and the comparative merit of the two classes will come fairly under consideration. But if the hold is trifling, and the hereditary right essentially at the mercy of the governing power, then the person in whom vested must be in constant dread of destruction; and, in consequence, be the mere creature of such power, administering to its aid in such manner as it pleases.

From this view it appears to me that the government of Lacedemon could not be considered as one which moved on the principle of distinct orders, or which derived its support from that source. The senate did not rest on that ground, nor could it resist the Assembly of the People in case of conflict, nor could the kings afford them any aid, for it was only as members of the senate that they had any share in the government. In time of war commanders of the troops were necessary, and they held that station by hereditary right, but it was distinct from and subordinate to the government and under its control. By what means then was the government supported for the term that it existed? We must look for these to other causes, and not to that to be derived from a balance between distinct orders, or the principle on which such government is founded.

The government of Athens was found to be an impracticable one, and it was made so by the union of the government with the sovereignty in the people, and the exercise of all the great powers of the government by the people collectively. All the objections then which apply to the Athenian government in those respects are equally applicable to the Lacedemonian. How happens it then that the government of Lacedemon was more permanently tranquil in its movement than that of Athens? Many causes contributed to that result, but the career and fate of the Athenian government alone afford all the demonstration on this point which can be desired by the most skeptical. Where the defects are the same, the remedy which saved the one government would save the other. To sustain the government of Athens, some expedient which should take the exercise of its powers out of the hands of the people collectively, and commit it by their consent to another party and make them the deluded instruments was indispensable. That expedient soon presented itself, and of which they availed themselves. It has been shown that about ten years after the government of Solon was instituted, the people suffered the power to be taken from them by Pisistratus, and actually aided him in the usurpation, and supported him in the exercise of it with occasional interruptions during his life, and as they thought in defense of their rights and of the constitution, though in direct violation of both. They were afterwards ruled by Miltiades, Themistocles,

Aristides, Pericles, and others, by their own consent. The people in General Assembly never ruled themselves by any arrangement of their own. Physicians administer drugs to cure diseases. The remedy is not pleasant, and a strong dose would often kill the patient. A moderate one affords relief.

If the defects of the government of Athens compelled the people of that state to resort to an expedient in actual subversion of the constitution, while the power remained in their hands ostensibly only, how much more natural was it for those of Lacedemon to avail themselves of a resource provided by the constitution itself, which should preserve the constitution and with it the powers to the exercise of which they were competent. The Senate of Lacedemon could not be an object of jealousy with the people, and consisting of fewer members than the Prytanean Corps which formed only one-tenth of that of Athens, was more capable of digesting and preparing measures to be proposed to the General Assembly of the People, and of executing all its other duties. Nor could the kings be an object of dread. Those people had always been subject to the rule of kings, and they enjoyed under the constitution of Lycurgus more freedom than they had ever experienced before. As senators, they certainly could not; and when called to the command of armies in time of war their hereditary quality in that station would give support to the General Assembly of the People in two important circumstances. By exciting a jealousy of their power and views it would unite the people more closely together: and by holding it in their own right the necessity to fill it by election, whereby contests between popular leaders for the command, the tendency of which always is in such a state of society and under a government so formed to divide the people into violent parties, and convulse, if not overthrow it, would be prevented.

The division of the regal power between two kings could not have failed to contribute much to reconcile the General Assembly of the People to the portion which they enjoyed, and to their agency in its concerns. The history of that state shows that it had an important influence on its fate at a very early period and in every subsequent stage. The constitution of Lycurgus was adopted, as has already been stated, about two hundred and fifty years before that of Solon, when the people of Greece generally, and especially those of the Peloponnesus had made but a slight progress in civilization. The tyrannies which had grown up in all the states, the offspring of the governments which had been formed in their most early and rude state, were overthrown except in Lacedemon. The preservation of monarchy in that state was owing to that cause, the division of the royal power between two kings, descendants of Hercules, but of different branches of that house. The rivalry and jealousy which existed between them and which descended to their successors weakened their power, and gave to the government a milder tone. Each to sustain himself and undermine his competitor courted popular favor, and thus the government was thrown more immediately on the people. The motive for a change was, therefore, less urgent in Lacedemon than in the other states, and to that cause it is presumed, it was owing that monarchy was not overthrown there at the same time that it was in the other states. It may fairly be inferred, therefore; that it continued to have a like effect after that constitution was adopted, and in the mode suggested.

There were other causes which must have contributed to secure to the Lacedemonian government a more tranquil movement and a longer existence than befell that of Athens. By the equal division of lands among the citizens, the opposite and conflicting classes of the rich and the poor could not exist among them. By messing together at public tables at common charge, they formed a species of company in which the interest of one was that of the whole. All domestic concerns of the most interesting nature became those of the public. By the education of their children by the state, every individual was made a public man, and by the substitution of iron for gold and silver as a currency, by the suppression of commerce and the discouragement of all intercourse with foreign nations by the more intelligent class of society on each side, the people were attached to and preserved in the rude state in which they then were, especially as all the great powers of the government were in principle in their hands and ostensibly so in practice.

There was another cause of a character equally marked which must have had a like effect. It appears from the history of Lacedemon, that the large crowds which were collected in the general assembly at every meeting became impatient, as those of Athens likewise did of the restraint imposed on them, to accept or reject without amendment the propositions which were sent to them by the senate, and that they often broke through it, and made such amendments as they thought fit. In this course the government moved on about one hundred and thirty years, the senate and the kings yielding to the pressure. At length they took alarm from a conviction that if those encroachments were not checked, and the constitution restored to its original state, their power would be annihilated. They made an effort to that effect, and succeeded in it; but to reconcile the people to it, they proposed an amendment to the constitution by the institution of the Ephori, which was adopted and which gave a new character to the government. This amendment was adopted at the particular suggestion of Theopompus, one of the then reigning kings, and as he avowed to preserve the power which he then held.

It cannot be doubted that the institution of this corps diminished considerably the cares and duties of the General Assembly of the People, and produced in other respects a very important effect on the fortune of the government. The members of the corps being elected by the people possessed the confidence of the General Assembly, and standing between that Assembly and the senate and kings, the natural tendency of its action was to take all the powers from the General Assembly which it could not discharge with advantage, and in the exercise of them to encroach on those of the senate and kings. The members of the corps would seek popularity with their constituents, which might be gained by exciting suspicions of the views of the other branches and by an unceasing pressure on them. In pursuit of this object some might not be over scrupulous as to the means, while others would be modest and honest, and perform their duty with perfect integrity. Zeal in the representative in defending the rights and promoting the interest of his constituents is correct and honorable, but the cause may be abused. It requires great knowledge of constitutional principles, and of the policy which a due regard to the public interest dictates, to fix the precise limit to which that zeal should be carried, and great firmness of nerve and loftiness of sentiment in moments of great public excitement to stem in any degree the current, and to stop at that point on the responsibility of the individual. Some will expose themselves to that hazard. Others will go with the current regardless of the consequences, be they what they may. I speak of man as he is and has always been.

The direct tendency of the powers vested in this corps would be to enable it by the exercise of them, should selfish motives be yielded to, to acquire in the progress of affairs all those of every other branch. Being elected annually by the people and considered as the defenders of their rights, it would take from the General Assembly by its consent all the powers which it could not discharge with advantage, which would leave it a very limited sphere of action. The opinion of that Assembly would be sought and be pursued by the corps, but the latter would constitute the efficient government, with the support of the former, which would be the instrument. The General Assembly being thus relieved by a corps of its own creation, from a dependence on the kings and senate for a performance of any of the duties to which it was incompetent, would not only cease to repose on the latter for any of those aids, but yield to and cherish the jealousy which the hereditary right of the one and long service of the other would naturally inspire. The Ephori would in consequence soon acquire the control of the kings and in a great measure of the senate, and thus have the whole government in its hands. Had the corps consisted of one member only, and he been vested with the right to command an army, or had that right been vested in the president of the corps, he would soon have usurped the government, making use of the people as his instruments; but there being five, and their powers being exclusively civil, all that they could accomplish would be to supplant by means thereof the plan of the General Assembly of the People, and impair the authority of the kings and senate.

The career of the Lacedemonian government corresponded after this corps was instituted with the view thus presented. It is attested by the highest authorities that by degrees it absorbed all the great powers of the government: that it had a censorship over the public morals, supervised the conduct of the magistrates and suspended them from office at pleasure; raised troops, gave orders to their commanders, interrupted them in victory, controlled their operations and recalled them from service, two of their body attending them in the field as spies on their conduct; that it received ambassadors from foreign powers, convened the General Assembly, scrutinized the conduct of the kings, summoned them before them to answer charges alleged against them; seized their persons, brought them to trial, and sometimes imposed fines on them by their own authority. Many of these powers belonged to the General Assembly of the People, and were exercised as may fairly be presumed, with their sanction and by their desire; the others were derived from encroachment on the senate and kings. By exercising them they supplied the defects of the one, and broke down the feeble barrier which the constitution had erected in defense of the others.

Whether the government could have sustained itself without the institution of the Ephori for the term it did, is a question of very serious, and I may add, of very doubtful import. How far the other regulations would have had that effect without the aid of that corps, must be matter of conjecture. Many writers of great distinction applaud in the highest degree the equal division of lands among the citizens, with the establishment of public repasts, and the education of children by the state. Polybius thinks that these regulations with a view to the liberty of the people and the safety of the state from foreign invasion, indicate a divine inspiration;[39] and other writers concur in that sentiment. I have no doubt, regarding the period at which that constitution was instituted, and the rude state of society at the time, that they had great effect in sustaining the government at that epoch, and in every subsequent stage while the society remained in that state. But still it is uncertain whether of themselves they would have been adequate to the object. My impression is that they would not. Under those regulations, with the aid of the kings and senate, in the manner, on the principle,

---

[41]Polybius, Vol. III. extract iii. chap. i.

and for the reasons stated, the government moved on in tolerable tranquility, one hundred and thirty years. In that interval, however, the General Assembly of the People manifested the discontent which was shown by the General Assembly of Athens, and which at the period adverted to had risen to such a height as to alarm the kings and senate and excite their opposition; the result of which was the institution of this corps at the instance of one of the kings for their safety. Had it not been instituted, it may fairly be presumed that the contentions which had commenced on that point would have been extended to others, and overthrown the government at a much earlier period. As soon as the friendly relation between the parties was broken, all ties between them would have ceased, and full force have been given to the defects of the system under aggravated circumstances. The institution of this corps restored tranquility to the state, and its powers in the commencement being rather of a negative than of a positive character, gaining on each side, and enlarging the sphere of action by the force of circumstances, it was thereby enabled to prevent any direct explosion, and to keep the machine in motion for a much longer term than it otherwise could have done.

This government in its organization, in the endowment of its branches, and in all its provisions and regulations was adapted to the rude state of society and none other. To that state the government was peculiarly suited, and to preserve it in that state the regulations specified were eminently well calculated. If the people were admitted into the government in that early age, whether it was in complete sovereignty, or in participation, it could only be en masse, or collectively, and if they preserved the power for any term especially, it could be only by availing themselves of extra or artificial aids, repugnant to the principle of the government, and adverse to their improvement in civilization. The defects of their power could not be cured by any provision consistent with it; and if such provision was carried beyond a very limited scope it would involve controversies which would be sure to subvert the government. No arrangement had ever been made to put the government in operation on the principle of distinct orders, in a manner to preserve a balance between them. It is thus that we account for the harmonious co-operation between the General Assembly of the People and the kings and senate. All the other provisions tended to keep the people in the rude state, and to support the government in its then form. The equal division of lands among the citizens, public repasts in which all messed together, kings, senators and laborers; the education of children by the state; the suppression of commerce; exclusion of foreigners; all had that tendency, as they had to keep affairs in their then state. Improve the society, civilize it, and the whole fabric would fall to pieces.

Had the government of Lacedemon rested on the same ground with that of Athens, on a General Assembly of the People and a numerous senate, and been left to itself without other aids, it would in my opinion have blown up at once as that of Athens did. If an edifice falls when certain props which rest against it are removed, the proof is complete that it was sustained by those props. Such too was the fate of the government of Lacedemon. By wars and other causes the state of the country was gradually changed. An intercourse took place with foreign nations. The door was opened to commerce. Iron was laid aside and gold and silver restored as the currency. The people became more civilized, and, in consequence, all those internal regulations which were adapted to the barbarous state were abandoned. The props which had sustained the government were removed and it fell of course.

CARTHAGE

THE government of Carthage is that next in order, according to the plan originally laid down, which claims attention. This people inhabited Africa, another quarter of the globe, and they afford the only example ever known in that quarter of a government which might be called free. The ruins of their city are still visible on the Mediterranean, near Tunis, and are often visited by travelers. No vestige or remnant of liberty is seen there. A perfect despotism prevails, and with it an ignorance and barbarism which exhibit man in the most degraded state.

In treating of a republican government in Africa we are led to inquire by what race of people it was instituted, what their origin, and the intermediate stages in their history which led to that result. No other portion of the people in that quarter could have instituted such a government, and had one been instituted for them it must have failed immediately by their utter inability to preserve it. The aborigines of Carthage were not Africans. The founders of the city emigrated from Tyre, in Phoenicia, a province of Syria. Their origin is traced to a far more remote source. The Phoenicians emigrated from Saboa, a part of Arabia, which borders on the eastern side of the Red Sea. The history of the Phoenicians and of the Saboans of whom they were a colony, the state of civilization which they had attained, with the causes which produced it, their emigration from Saboa to Syria, and of a portion of their population thence along the Mediterranean to Carthage, with the different stages in this progress, is intimately connected with the history of the eastern world. It is nevertheless certain, that taken in its greatest extent, including the rise and fall of empires in that quarter, with the state of science, commerce, and the arts, so far as it is known, it sheds little light on the subject on which I treat. It is generally admitted that Egypt and Asia are the countries which were first settled, since in going back to the earliest records of time and comparing them with other countries, with Greece for example, we find the population there much greater than with them, and improvements in civilization and the arts generally more advanced. Emigrants from Egypt and Asia to Greece introduced commerce, agriculture, alphabetical writing, and some knowledge of the arts among the people. But what was the state of that epoch on each side? The Greeks were altogether rude and uncivilized. The Egyptians and Asiatics, the Phoenicians particularly, somewhat advanced beyond them. The improvement of the Greeks, though gradual and slow was great, while that of the eastern nations has remained in the state in which it then was.

The origin of Asia, and of Egypt, the only part of Africa which merits attention in the view under consideration, compared with that of Greece and the European states generally is little known, and what we do know of it is derived almost altogether from Greek and Roman authors. The accounts which those writers give of those people represent them at the most distant ages known, essentially in the state in which they now are, as very populous communities; despotism with great wealth and splendor at the head; slavery with ignorance, poverty, and wretchedness among the people. The opposite classes in society were separated at a vast distance from each other, and which could have been produced only by the great age of those communities, and other causes which tend in the progress of time to promote inequality among the people. When communities reach that state, improvement in their governments in favor of the rights of the people, with corresponding checks on the power of the crown becomes extremely difficult, and must be attended with convulsion. If the people have not acquired an improvement in intelligence and other circumstances to render them capable of discharging the duties and sustaining the station thus obtained, these efforts must fail, or terminate in the case of change, in the transfer only of the power from the existing circumstances to some leader, and thus form the commencement of a new dynasty over them. In this state Asia and Africa, with the exception of Phoenicia in the former, and of Carthage in the Phoenician colony in the latter, have been always known to modern times, according to the best accounts which have been transmitted to us.

The government of Carthage resembled that of Athens in the two most important features. The sovereignty was in the people, and the government united with the sovereignty; but in many of its modifications it essentially varied from it. It consisted of a General Assembly of the People; of a Senate; and of two magistrates, who were called Suffetes. the Senators were elected by the people, as were the Suffetes. The number of members of which the Senate was composed is unknown. Their term of service was for life. The Suffetes were elected annually.

The people in General Assembly had the power to elect the magistrates, to regulate the finances, to make peace and war, and to form alliances in the mode prescribed by the constitution.

Every individual born of parents, both of whom were citizens, was a citizen. The revenue, to be eligible to office, was prescribed. Every citizen was an elector.

From the Senate two corps of councils were formed, one consisting of one hundred and four members, and the other of five. Those of the first held their offices for life. Those of the second for a term only: the precise length of which is unknown.

The Suffetes had a right to convene the Senate, to propose to it subjects for deliberation, and to take the votes of the members. They presided in the tribunals and were agents-general of the republic. They likewise sometimes commanded the armies. On retiring from that office they became Pretors, in which character they had a right to propose new laws, and to call to account those who were charged with the administration of the public finances.

The powers of the Senate were very extensive. Its decrees had the form of laws when the vote was unanimous. In case of a division the proposition was sent to the Assembly of the People. The vote of a single member in opposition produced that result. When the proposition was submitted to the people, they were not compelled to adopt or reject it as presented, but had a right to dispose of it as they thought fit.

The Council of One Hundred and Four was called the Council of Ancients, and charged with the superintendence of the constituted authorities, and particularly of the conduct of the generals and admirals of the republic. It was considered the guardian of the constitution. The Council of Five had likewise extensive powers. They appointed their colleagues when vacancies occurred, and likewise the members of the Council of One Hundred and Four, into which body they returned, when their term of services had expired.

Such was the government of Carthage, according to the best information that I have been able to obtain from the works of Aristotle, Polybius, Livy, and Diodorus Siculus, among the ancients, and such modern writers as I have had access to. Aristotle bestowed on it a very high commendation. It had existed when he wrote about five hundred years, during which, he observes, that the state had never been disturbed by sedition, nor had the liberties of the people been menaced by a tyrant. He considered it as one of the most perfect constitutions that had been known. For this tranquility very satisfactory causes may be assigned. The example of the governments of Athens and Lacedemon furnishes them.

The great causes to which the overthrow of the Athenian government was imputable, were the union of the government with the sovereignty, and the exercise of the powers of the government by the people collectively.

It was the inability of the people to perform the duties of a government in that manner, which enabled Pisistratus to wrest it from them and to exercise its powers in his own right, and which made them after his overthrow mere instruments in the hands of popular leaders. It was the same cause which induced the people of Lacedemon to acquiesce in the power of the Senate and kings, by whom many of those duties were performed, the discharge of which by them collectively would have overthrown it. In the government of Carthage the arrangement was the same on principle that it was in the Athenian; the government was united with the sovereignty in the people, to be exercised by them collectively, or en masse, but such was the arrangement, that they could scarcely ever be called on to act in that form. Whenever the vote of the Senate was unanimous, the question was decided. A reference to the people became unnecessary, and such was the organization of the Senate, that while it was calculated to inspire confidence in the people, it remedied in a considerable degree the defects of a body thus constituted. The great number of which it was composed enabled it to form a kind of substitute for the General Assembly of the People, and thus to prevent their discontent. Incapable of discharging the duties themselves, they would readily yield their place to so large a portion of their mass whom they had elected. And the defects inseparable from so numerous a body as the Senate in the discharge of the powers vested in it, were mitigated by the duties which were performed by the Council of One Hundred and Four, which was composed of members of the Senate, and likewise by the Council of Five, who were taken from the One Hundred and Four. All writers agree that the powers vested in these two councils were great, and which cannot be doubted, as it may fairly be inferred that every measure, legislative as well as executive, originated with that of the Five, and after being prepared were submitted by them to the whole body of the Senate. In this mode it seems as if the best provisions which such an organization admitted of, were adopted to remedy the great defects of the system.

The great difference between the government of Carthage, and that of Athens, consisted in the following circumstances. By the constitution of Athens no measure could be adopted without the sanction of the General Assembly of the People, and for this purpose they were convened regularly every month, and frequently several times in a month. By the constitution of Carthage no proposition of any kind was submitted to the people when the vote of the Senate was unanimous. The whole business of the state was managed in that event by the Senate, and the councils formed by its members, and by the Suffetes. This principle being established, it may be presumed that appeals were seldom made to the people, and were avoided, except in cases of great emergency, in accord with the wishes of both bodies, the General Assembly and the Senate. The incompetency of the people to perform the duties of a government, in General Assembly, would reconcile them to the performance of them by the other bodies, especially as they would be taken from the pursuits of industry, received no compensation for the service, and those who did perform them took their appointments from their suffrage. It is equally presumable that the Senate would harmonize in such a policy, and be glad both from personal and public considerations to be freed from the embarrassment that would attend frequent meetings of the whole people, and the control by them in General Assembly of all the measures of the state. To avoid such embarrassment it would be natural in the transaction of the business that an understanding should be formed among the members, even before the discussion of any proposition, what the sentiment of the majority respecting it would be; and that the minority would accommodate with it. It does not appear that regular meetings on fixed days in each month were provided for, and special duties assigned to each, as was done by the constitution of Athens, and would be necessary if the government was to be managed by the people, or depended uniformly on their sanction. The appeal to them being contingent, even in the most important cases, makes this view the more presumable.

What then sustained the government for such a length of time, and with such tranquility and contentment among the people? What produced a like effect with the government and people of Lacedemon when the Senate consisted comparatively of a few members, and the kings were hereditary? The great causes were essentially the same in each instances. The people were attached to liberty, and being incompetent to its preservation by the discharge of the duties of the government themselves, collectively, and incapable of instituting any other, they acquiesced in the performance of a large portion of those duties by other powers, retaining in their own hands with the sovereignty those only to which they were more competent. The division of land among the citizens with public repasts in Lacedemon, it may be presumed, contributed much to reconcile the people of that state to the commission of the power to so small a Senate, and likewise to the hereditary quality of the kings. How long could such a system be preserved, and what were the causes which would be sure to overthrow it? In tracing these I shall not advert to casual events to which all governments and people are subject, and which produce great changes in the communities in which they occur. While the morals and intelligence of the people remain unchanged, and no pressure is made from abroad which menaces to overwhelm them, their acquiescence with the government in its existing state would probably continue. If the morals of the people should become corrupted they would be incapable of sustaining the station they held in the government, and sink under a tyrant. Or if any cause occured which should induce the people to take a more active part in the administration; to assume powers to which they were incompetent; such as were exercised by the people of Athens, and which produced the overthrow of their government, a like fate would befall the government of Carthage. This might happen while the morals of the people remain unchanged, and their attachment to liberty equally great. Instances might occur in which those who managed the affairs of the state excite the distrust and even the indignation of the people. Wars, for example, might be undertaken imprudently, which might by ill-success menace their independence. If the people had borne the existing government as the only means of preserving their liberties, the bond between them and those who wielded it, would be slight. It must have been of a nature compulsory rather than confidential. Under such circumstances it would be incumbent on a virtuous people, attached to liberty, to exert all their faculties to preserve it. Convulsions might ensue, which might be productive of the most fatal consequences.

FINIS

INDEX

125

sovereign. As the American Republic enters its third century, such injunctions ought not to be ignored."

RUSSELL KIRK, a man of letters, is the Editor of *The University Bookman*. He is the author of more than 20 books, among them *Eliot and His Age, John Randolph of Roanoke, The Political Principles of Robert A. Taft, Roots of American Order, Edmund Burke*, and *Decadence and Renewal in Higher Learning*. His column on education appeared in *National Review* for two decades, and both *Time* and *Newsweek* have described him as one of America's leading thinkers. His pioneering study on *The Conservative Mind*, now in its 7th edition, is widely regarded as the principal catalyst of the modern conservative movement.